FUNDRAISING:

Engaging Your Community

James D. Klote

Harcover ISBN: 979-8-218-18721-7

Paperback ISBN: 979-8-218-18722-4

eBook ISBN: 979-8-218-18723-1

CONTENTS

This book is dedicated to the pioneers
of charitable fundraising in the United States;
Charles S. Ward (1859-1929),
Christian H. Dreshman (1880-1955),
and Herman F. Reinhardt (1893-1964).

As President of Ward, Dreshman & Reinhardt, Inc.,
I take great pride in our 110-year history and over 8,000 Capital Campaigns.
It is an honor to carry on the tradition of these fine men.

ABOUT THE AUTHOR

How did you get involved in fundraising consulting?

After I graduated from college, I took a position with the United Way in Columbus, Ohio. I proved that I had a talent for rallying support for a cause and motivating people to accomplish a shared goal. After a few years with the United Way, I was recruited by Ward, Dreshman & Reinhardt (WD&R), the country's oldest and most prestigious fundraising consulting firm. At twenty-six, I was the youngest consultant the firm had ever hired.

Is it true that you became president of WD&R when you were only thirty-two?

It is true, and it is still amazing to me that I became president at such a young age. The company has a long and storied history; it was established in 1890 and was a founding tenant in the Empire State Building and then in Rockefeller Center. When I was hired, I was the consummate company man. I went anywhere I was sent, to any campaign, no questions asked, and I got results. After a few years of that, the executives also realized that I had a talent for selling the WD&R service, mostly because I believed so deeply in the Plan of Campaign, if executed properly. Becoming president of WD&R was incredibly humbling. I was able to work with and lead men and women who had previously mentored me. It was a challenge and a great opportunity.

Why did you create James D. Klote & Associates (JDK&A)? What was the purpose?

For over a hundred years, WD&R has directed Capital Campaigns for a variety of institutions, including hospitals, schools, churches, and nearly every sector of nonprofit, from athletics to arts organizations to libraries. I was always curious about what prospective clients thought of our ability to raise funds for churches as well as sporting arenas. After a few years with the firm, I began lobbying the firm's officers to create a division within WD&R to distinguish between secular and religious clients. The members of the board of WD&R and I decided it was important to distinguish the work we do as a firm for hospitals, schools, libraries, and arts organizations from the work we perform on behalf of individual churches and church-affiliated projects.

During our 1999 board meeting, I requested that we establish a division of the company that specifically focused on church Capital Campaigns. At that meeting, the board made a unanimous decision to do so and named the division James D. Klote & Associates. It was an incredible honor to have my name attached to such a project, as the services we provide to churches remain unmatched by any consulting firm in the United States.

Was the new division an immediate success?

It was easier to create a division that was associated with the country's oldest fundraising firm than it would have been to start an entirely new firm. In addition, using the name James D. Klote & Associates made the venture far easier, as I was already established in the industry and was relatively well known by clergy around the country. The other reason the establishment of the new division was less challenging than it might otherwise have been was because we continued to offer the full-time and on-site service we have offered as WD&R for over a hundred years. Clients could feel confident that they were getting the same high level of service and dedication from our staff that they had grown accustomed to over the years.

Who are the current clients of WD&R?

Today, we carry on the rich history of WD&R and JDK&A with a focus on personal attention and on-site Capital Campaign management. Currently, our specialty areas of focus are community nonprofit organizations, which include hospitals, schools, libraries, and other community efforts throughout the United States and Canada.

How has the global pandemic affected fundraising in the United States?

All around the world, COVID-19 has been the primary focus for the past couple of years. The pandemic has affected every aspect of our lives on a daily basis. Fundraising, and the support of all nonprofit organizations, are just one aspect of life that has been altered by the pandemic. The need to raise funds has not changed. Only the method by which we conduct fundraising campaigns and the way we engage constituents has needed to adapt. The demand for funding has only increased, as has the demand for the services of firms like ours that assist these nonprofit organizations. The fundamentals of our approach have not changed. What has changed is the manner in which we engage our constituents and donors. Use of technologies like Zoom has been instrumental in continuing our communications with these groups. In this book, I explain the many changes to successful fundraising

Why should any institution consider using the services of WD&R or JDK&A?

Our firm offers something that is unique in Capital Campaign consultation. We continue to *only* provide full-time and on-site consulting. Most organizations employ staff for the duration of annual campaigns and special purpose giving. However, these individuals are usually so focused on supporting these annual needs that they have little time to devote to a multimillion-dollar Capital Campaign. Utilizing the services of our firm eliminates the necessity for the current staff to devote their time to Capital Campaign efforts. When we are engaged as a firm, we essentially become part of the client's staff, and we are with them every step of the way. Our services include pre-campaign planning, Readiness Assessments, and Capital Campaign direction.

Why is this such a successful model for nonprofit organizations?

I had served on the board of trustees for one institution at Yale University. For many years prior, I served on the board of another in Washington, DC. The reason these institutions are so financially successful is because they take a deliberate approach to fundraising. These institutions engage their constituencies and create ownership in their programs and services. We offer this same approach at WD&R. In today's world, there is strong competition for charitable dollars. Tired old tactics such as mailing out pledge cards simply will not get the results that we do. This is why our approach is successful and it is why our clients are able to build new facilities, retire debt, and fund deferred maintenance on their buildings.

What do you see for yourself in the future?

I see more of the same. I am not going anywhere. I can't imagine a more rewarding career. Every day, I am thrilled and excited to be doing what I am doing. I also see no way around continuing to grow the firm. The number of requests we get for service increases exponentially every year. Name recognition is important, and Ward, Dreshman & Reinh has a long history of satisfied clients and successful campaigns. Likewise, James D. Klote & Associates, Inc. has its own roster of successful fundraising and Capital Campaigns. Both companies learn from each other and the combined knowledge base of both WD&R and JDK&A staff is unparalleled. The future looks bright.

If someone wishes to inquire about your services or ask about a position in your firm after reading your book, what is the best way to contact you?

All of our information is on our website at www.wdrincorp.com. I am always happy to share my insight into a fundraising situation, so I would encourage people to contact me if they are interested in our services for a Capital Campaign or are looking for ways to improve their annual campaigns. Certainly, if this type of service appeals to the reader and is something they think they might like to do, I would encourage anyone to contact my office. Additionally, prospective church clients can visit our JDK&A website at www.jdklote.com.

PREFACE

I have written this book because I am passionate about helping nonprofit organizations achieve their financial goals and building needs. This task has grown even greater due to the economic challenges our economy has suffered over the past couple of years during the pandemic. If you are considering a campaign effort for your institution, this book is required reading. It will help you understand the complexities of a capital campaign during this challenging time, introduce you to issues surrounding the selection of a consulting firm, and give you insight into problems you haven't considered yet. This book will lay out the map for you, but it is only a plan. A successful capital campaign requires proper implementation through experienced guidance. You only have one opportunity to conduct your campaign properly. Make sure you are working with a consulting firm that takes its job as seriously as you take yours. Shortcuts will never give you the results you need and can often lead to terrible mistakes. The business landscape in our communities has changed dramatically. Although this book contains detailed information and some may believe they can use it as a plan of campaign without engaging the services of a consulting firm, that is certainly not the intent. This is not a how-to manual for directing a capital campaign on your own. Rather, this book is designed to illustrate how complex the issues related to conducting a campaign can be and why professional help is required for you to be successful. Further, this book is designed to help you make the best decision for your organization when choosing a consulting firm to manage your capital campaign.

This book offers a path to engage your board, past donors, local businesses, and community leaders. As with all capital campaigns, buy-in from your constituency is crucial. This book explains how best to garner support for your campaign and identify groups that truly matter.

Why would I write a book on such a specialized topic and seemingly give away the secrets to true fundraising success? That is a question that my consultants and I at Ward, Dreshman & Reinhardt, Inc. and James D. Klote & Associates, Inc. have grappled with for years. Over time, we came to a consensus that this information needs to be shared. Now that a global pandemic has altered our way of life and affected our economy, it is even more crucial to share the right way for organizations to conduct fundraising in their communities. Part of our mission is to educate. Those very institutions that seek to do the same and to give back to their community are too often forgotten or left in the dark when it comes to fundraising expertise. Unfortunately, nonprofit organizations seem to learn lessons the hard way. With so many people, staff, and operational issues to worry about, campaigns are often pushed to the back burner, and knowledge of campaigns passes through storytelling and folklore rather than in codified tried and true best practices. I felt that it was my duty to put something in writing to help nonprofit organizations make better decisions regarding fundraising.

First and foremost, nonprofit leaders must understand the institution and envision the direction in which the organization needs to go after the worst of the pandemic has subsided. One of the most important things to consider when embarking on a capital campaign is to understand what your vision is for your organization. How has that vision been altered because of the lasting effects of COVID-19? Do you want to fund a new construction project? Would your community benefit from a renovation program? Would you use the money from a capital campaign to upgrade the infrastructure of your organization's headquarters or build a new facility? Are there other things your organization needs that it does not currently have? Does the organization have debt that is affecting annual programs and needs? These are all important questions to consider when beginning to think about your capital campaign. You must think about your constituents—your supporters and your staff—to determine where the funds raised from your capital campaign will go. Keep your organization's mission and vision in mind to ensure that you are properly focused on your campaign.

My firm offers a proven fundraising method that engages an organization's total constituency and community. Our approach to fundraising dates back to 1905, the year our firm was founded. For over a hundred years, our firm and our clients have worked together through some of the most challenging times in our history, including the Spanish Flu, the Great Depression, two world wars, and many, many national financial challenges. I have used this plan throughout my career as a consultant; any organization can utilize the same plan to maximize its fundraising potential. This plan was not designed overnight; it is the result of over one hundred years of service and the experience of running thousands of campaigns. This method is tested and proven. It works, even in times of crisis. I offer this plan in this book for one reason: it works. The true stories I share throughout the book illustrate the lessons I have learned so that you do not have to learn them for yourself. There's no need to reinvent the wheel; learn from my experience instead. When we share what we know, everyone benefits. I generalized the stories so that no particular person or organization could be identified. The organization in which the lesson was learned is not as important as the lesson itself. I don't intend to sound boastful; the stories are merely a reflection of my experience, and the success is born out of real campaigns. I find the same types of problems in every nonprofit campaign, and I am fortunate to be able to draw on my experience to solve them. Over the years, I have found that there is one way to conduct a capital campaign correctly, but there are a million ways to mess it up.

As the first and oldest capital campaign consulting firm in the country, WD&R has had the opportunity to present our plan to thousands of nonprofit organizations considering campaigns. In addition to WD&R, these organizations typically interview one or two part-time firms for the project. Years ago, when WD&R was not selected to conduct campaigns, I followed up with the organizations to find out why. Inevitably, the reason we were not chosen was the cost of our service. For a short time, I considered offering less a expensive, part-time service so that we might win more clients. I toyed with the idea and mentioned it to my wife one evening. She was surprised and told me that she didn't think I could do that because she knew that deep down, I did not believe in part-time service. She also knew that ultimately, if I didn't do what I believed was right for these organizations, I would be unhappy and my career would suffer. Instead of offering less comprehensive and less expensive service, she convinced me that I needed to demonstrate to the organizations that full-time, on-site capital campaign consulting was worth the investment. She was right, and WD&R continues to offer only full-time consulting service. I believe our track record speaks for itself.

Over the years, I have been contacted far too often by organizations that needed me to help them salvage a campaign after they had tried to conduct it on their own or had used an inferior method to save some money. In the end, it always ended up costing them more money. After my help, these organizations understand the concept of return on investment. However, the damage is often so severe that WD&R can be of no more assistance than to encourage them to allow a period of time to go by and then begin again, correctly. Organizations must wait for the ship to right itself before attempting to sail again. Unfortunately, this waiting period can last for years. Now that we have been challenged with life during a pandemic, it is even more crucial that a personalized and deliberate approach be followed. Those organizations that continue to rely on telemarketing and direct mail campaigns for fundraising will suffer greatly. I have always told clients that a personalized approach will fare better and be more successful than requests by telephone or mail. It is now even more important to rely on the personal touch, as charitable dollars may be more difficult to raise. Competition for donations is fierce and those organizations engaged in passive approaches may not survive in a post-pandemic economy. I have also stopped counting the number of times executive directors, administrators, and board members have told me I should teach this practical approach to nonprofit organization fundraising. They know it is proven and that it identifies and recruits the right organizational leaders to ensure an effective and productive campaign experience. This strategy is valuable. I hope this book will begin that education process.

The central theme to any capital campaign needs to be engaging with your constituency. Fundraising is more than just asking for money; it is a process of encouraging a renewed sense of commitment to the organization. Most likely, you have not had to physically build the building for which you are raising money—though if you have, this method is equally effective. I challenge every campaign committee to imagine what it would cost to build the organization if it was not already there. In most cases, you are merely renovating what others have built. One client I worked with on a capital campaign called this process of fundraising "standing on the shoulders of giants," and I think that sentiment captures the idea and imagination of the generational connection that nonprofit organizations want to engender in their community. People count on their hospitals, schools, libraries, and other nonprofit institutions to be great. They instill a sense of pride and spirit of service in the community. Shouldn't your campaign take those responsibilities into consideration?

I appreciate you taking the time to read my book on fundraising for nonprofit organizations during this challenging time in our nation's history. These are unparalleled times. However, as with my other published books and in all the services we provide for our clients, this book was a labor of love. I so enjoy what I do that I do not consider it work; it is my calling. I am very fortunate in so many areas of my life, including my wife, Molly; my children, Philip, Andrew, and Meredith; my many campaign consultants; the many clients and board members, administrators, and other business and community leaders whom I now call friends; and my ability to participate in and contribute to the lives of so many impactful nonprofit institutions.

—Jim Klote

CHAPTER 1
A History of Our Proven Approach
to Fundraising

Truly unique among capital fundraising companies, our firm paved the way for resident-directed methods of capital campaign consulting. We have remained on the leading edge of the industry since the company's founding in 1905. For over a hundred years, WD&R has worked with clients in both the for-profit and nonprofit sectors to successfully raise the necessary funds to continue the mission of each client organization. In 1883, Charles S. Ward, upon graduating from Dartmouth, began his career as general secretary of the Young Men's Christian Association (YMCA) of Lexington, Kentucky. Over the next two decades, Ward served in the same capacity for the YMCA's of New Britain, Connecticut; Grand Rapids, Michigan; and Minneapolis, Minnesota. The originator and developer of the short-term, organized, intensive method of campaigns for philanthropic causes and institutions, Ward spent most of his time at the various YMCA's raising money to keep the doors open.

In Grand Rapids, Ward approached the YMCA's board of directors and requested that they create an organized campaign effort tasked solely with paying for the YMCA's expenses over a long period of time. The campaign was to be an intensive, organized plan that would take place over a short time frame. In exchange, Ward agreed not to request additional funding from the board. The board agreed, and Ward's plan became so effective that YMCA organizations all across the United States began requesting

Ward's assistance with their own funding plans. In 1898, Ward was appointed field secretary of the YMCA and began assisting YMCA's in various cities and towns to raise funds for operations.

In 1905, Ward founded the firm, which still carries his name today. That same year, Ward took his principles and procedures for short-term, intensive, organized fundraising to Washington, DC, where he implemented the final phase of the fiftieth anniversary campaign for the Washington YMCA. Over the course of thirty days, the Ward-directed campaign was able to raise the remaining $85,000 necessary to conclude the appeal.

Between 1905 and 1915, countless organizations sought the expertise of Charles S. Ward, including the YMCA's of London and Edinburgh and the first-ever campaign for a hospital in 1911 in Salem, Ohio.

In 1914, Ward adapted his fundraising techniques to conducting capital campaigns for colleges and universities, and in 1916, Ward directed an American Red Cross nationwide membership campaign, increasing membership from 22,500 to 31,000,000. At the conclusion of the membership drive in 1917, the American Red Cross had raised $123 million through Ward's efforts. The following year, in 1918, Ward led a second nationwide capital campaign for the Red Cross, raising more than $181 million.

Chris Dreshman, an early associate of Charles S. Ward, joined the firm in 1920 after serving as the downtown secretary for the YMCA of Pittsburgh—one of Ward's former clients. Dreshman ultimately became chairman of the board in 1929 and continued directing the firm until his death in 1955. Along with eight other leaders of fundraising firms, Dreshman formed the American Association of Fund-Raising Counsel to establish the professional and ethical standards required for fundraising. During his thirty-five-year tenure with the WD&R, Dreshman personally directed forty campaigns for educational institutions throughout the United States.

In 1930, Herman Reinhardt joined the firm, where he served until his death in 1964. He was a noted leader and innovator for major fundraising causes for educational institutions, YMCA's, the Red Cross, and several major hospitals. Reinhardt regarded each of his firm's commitments as a personal one, establishing deep and enduring relationships with each client. Reinhardt won the deep respect of business and community leaders throughout the country for his high ideals. During Reinhardt's tenure, Ward, Dreshman & Reinhardt relocated from the iconic Empire State Building, where the firm was a founding tenant, to the world-famous Rockefeller Center.

These early successes, rooted in a foundation of mission-driven capital campaign consulting, serve as the backbone of the successful organization that WD&R became and remains to this day. In the firm's 110-year history, WD&R has directed nearly eight thousand capital campaigns, raising over $3 billion.

Today, WD&R concentrates its services on nonprofit organizations and schools. The accumulated experience of our campaign directors, combined with innovators carefully field-tested and judiciously applied, provides a unique perspective for today's capital campaign efforts. At WD&R, we believe that our unique blend of personal service and professional experience is the main reason why our firm has been the leading capital campaign consulting firm in the United States for the past century.

Our specialty is providing full-time, on-site fundraising counsel for nonprofit organizations. Our full-time approach combines personal attention and a proven method of successful fundraising. The WD&R director relocates to your community for the duration of the campaign, thereby giving him or her a front-row seat to all phases and aspects of the campaign. The campaign director provides your organization with full-time access to our expertise and guidance. Meetings are planned to meet the schedule of your volunteers, problems are addressed immediately, extensive coaching of campaign workers is provided, campaign progress is monitored closely, preparation of campaign materials are designed on-site for the approval of the client, and weekly progress reports are submitted to the appropriate leaders.

We pledge to serve only those voluntary, philanthropically supported causes whose purposes are to advance the needs of all humanity; organize and conduct these campaigns on the highest possible level; and recommend only that which, as indicated by our long and successful experience, is in the best interest of our clients.

It is our goal at WD&R to ensure that your organization has comprehensive, continual support before, during, and after your capital campaign. Using our hundred-plus years of experience, we are dedicated to guiding your organization through the complicated process of a capital campaign, ensuring the most successful outcome. We do not take our history or our responsibilities to the capital campaign process lightly and we strive to provide you with only the highest level of full-time, on-site service to make your fundraising dreams a reality. It is truly our pleasure to bring WD&R's experience to bear on your campaign. We can't wait to get started.

CHAPTER 2
Understanding Your Organization

Soul Searching

Who are you?

If you are reading this book, you are likely involved in some aspect of fundraising or development for your nonprofit organization. Undoubtedly, the global pandemic has made your job much more challenging. Whether you are a member of the board, administration, prospective donor, or simply a concerned constituent, the lessons in this book should serve as a guide to help you in your fundraising efforts. Perhaps you are new to the organization and you see great, untapped potential all around you. Maybe you see the children or adults who are involved in your organization and you have a burning desire to make your nonprofit all that it can be so that it can provide them with the best possible experience. Or perhaps you have been involved with the organization for years and you know that there is more you could be doing to provide the best service and experience possible. Perhaps you believe you are not doing enough—or that you already do too much. Raising funds for a nonprofit organization can be difficult. Often, you have already asked the same people over and over again to give of their time and talents. In response, they have risen to the occasion and selflessly worked on fundraising efforts with you. But you are wary of asking the same people for help yet again. How do you begin to decide what to do? How do you decide where to allocate funds raised, whether it is to encourage more programs or recruit more people to the board or administration? How do you know what your constituents want or need? This is the place to start. We start by beginning to answer these questions and exploring what your organization is and whom you serve. Knowing that will make the rest of this process that much easier.

What kind of a nonprofit organization are you?

Demographics:

What does your organization specialize in? How has the pandemic affected your mission? Are you a hospital involved in health care throughout the community? A Chamber of Commerce dedicated to business and community development? Or a different sector of nonprofit? How many people are employed by and involved in your organization? What ages do you serve? Can your organization account for any recent accomplishments that might attract new accreditations or get the attention of additional constituents and prospective donors? Are you open and available to everyone in your community?

Location:

Is your organization located in a rural or urban area? How do people get to your organization? How does your organization fit in with your community, and how do your constituents or members engage with the surrounding area? What does the community think about your organization? Does your organization fill an important role in the community? For instance, do you offer health care, public service, personal development, shelter space, or artistic performances that are open to the public? How does your organization add value to the community?

Style:

How is your organization perceived by the community? Is it traditional, progressive, welcoming, or educational? Can you reach out to local business and community leaders for support by virtue of the effect your organization has in the community? Has the organization's mission remained consistent since you arrived, or has it changed over time? Have you personally changed? Has your approach to serving the organization changed?

Communication:

How well do your staff, members, and constituents know each other? Is it easy for someone to contact the organization leaders with questions? Do members of the community feel comfortable reaching out to the administration or board with concerns? Do you ever sponsor an organization-wide event to bring all stakeholders together? Do members volunteer for activities outside of business hours? What do the staff, board, and members of the community think of the organization? How do you know? When was your last board meeting and who attended? Who didn't attend and why? What was discussed? Do you find that you only hear from stakeholders when something is wrong? Do you receive positive feedback on organizational operations? Do your stakeholders talk to you about their dreams and ambitions for the organization?

Development:

If you are one of the leaders of the organization, such as the executive director or administrator, are you involved in the development committee and the process of fundraising? If not, why not? Who is in charge of fundraising efforts and activities? How are your fundraising activities decided upon and conducted? Do you publicize your fundraising events or campaigns? How have your events changed because of COVID-19? If your fundraising schedule only occurs once during the year, when does it occur? Do you try to capitalize on holiday giving by raising funds during the winter months? Do you send a letter to members of the community asking for their help? Do you engage the business leaders in the community? What percentage of your funds raised come from traditional donors? Are you able to build your constituency each year with new donors? Do you anticipate being able to do so even in light of the pandemic? Who is involved in the campaign efforts? Is the administration involved? Is there a committee of past presidents or board members you can turn to for guidance? Is person-to-person visitation or outreach encouraged? How do you communicate with the community about fundraising necessities or campaigns?

Does your organization publish a budget that is freely available? Does anyone read it, other than to review staff salaries? Does the administration or board shy away from the topic of finances to focus on program development? Are all potential donors treated equally and respectfully when asked to contribute? Is the focus on equal opportunity for participation, not equal giving?

Is your organizational program progressive or traditional? What methods have you implemented to ensure that the members of your community are getting the best possible experience?

Do you have enough staff? Are you drowning in paperwork? Are you able to accommodate each member of the community who has needs or wants to participate in the organization? Is the organization limited due to space constraints, staffing issues, or lack of funding? Does the board fully support all the objectives and current goals of the organization? Are you trying to do too much? How do you receive feedback on your decisions regarding the organization?

Facilities:

What is the state of your facilities and infrastructure? Are you able to make necessary repairs and renovations when needed to keep your organization safe? If you were faced with a surprise repair tomorrow—for example, damage from a hurricane or a collapsed roof caused by snow—would your budget be able to absorb the hit? When was the physical location for your organization built? Do you keep it up to date and maintained? When was the last renovation to your building, if ever? Is the facility in disrepair, or is it a model for your community?

Is your organization pleasing and welcoming, or merely functional and adequate? Do members of the community enjoy coming to your organization or do they consider the facilities or location something they have to endure? Is the organization handicapped accessible? If you wanted to expand your space, could you? Do you have restrictions on expansion? For instance, if you wanted to expand either facilities or parking, do you have the space? Would you need to acquire additional property on which to expand?

Finances:

It is important to understand the steps necessary to raise the money you need while also paying off debt. Three years ago, I worked with a client who initially wanted to conduct a building campaign. Part of that campaign was ridding the organization of approximately $5 million in debt. However, the organization dragged its feet and did not do its due diligence; they did not even conduct a feasibility study to determine the support of the needs and projected outcome of their fundraising. Recently, the client called me. His organization was in real crisis; in addition to a desperate need for new facilities, the debt had more than quintupled to over $20 million. The campaign's focus became debt reduction, which is not as glamorous as a building effort. Even though the campaign raised significant funds, all they could do was pay off the debt.

Are you in debt supporting your current programs and curriculum? Do you have an endowment? Do you really want one? Do you have any other assets?

An organization that I worked with was left a sizable endowment by a member who had passed away. They were thrilled that this individual remembered them in the will. Initially, the endowment served as a way to back small loans, which were then paid off quickly. The principal was never touched. Years went by and a new administrator was hired by the board. Many of the organization's leadership changed positions and few board members were able to clearly remember who had given the original endowment or why. As time passed, the organization needed many things. The board members considered the pros and cons of taking out loans versus using the principal of the endowment or conducting a fundraising campaign to pay for necessary repairs and desired renovation programs. Nearly everyone was in agreement that the institution should spend the principal of the endowment, but a member of the community approached the board members and asked why this course of action was being considered. The board chair told the man that this was an easier path than conducting a campaign as the money already existed; it would not need to be raised. The man protested, "Do you really think that this is why these funds were left to the institution? The endowment was left as a testament of the donor's desire for the institution to remain financially independent. If he knew it would end up being the cause of laziness among the next generation of leaders, I am certain he would not have left it." The board chair considered the man's concerns and addressed the board with these sentiments. After careful consideration, the board decided to proceed with a capital campaign. The members worked diligently and were able to raise significant funds. Today, they still enjoy the security of their endowment and have a financial buffer for unforeseen events because of their foresight.

This is an important lesson to remember, as many institutions are fortunate to have endowments. But care should always be taken when deciding when and where to spend that money.

Now that you have read through that seemingly endless list of questions and have considered your own situation, take a moment to imagine your vision for your organization if money were no object. Imagine not only what you need, but also what you want. What new facilities would you build? What new initiatives would you consider? Who else in the community could you serve? How could you provide your business and community members with the best experience possible?

Vision:

Is your organization merely about one particular focus in the community or are you also interested in expanding your services? What are your goals for the members of your constituency and prospective donors? Do you need to change the type of organization you are if you are to accomplish your goals and adhere to your mission? Have you become exclusive rather than inclusive for any number of reasons? Are you limited by enrollment or by other, financial factors? Is the organization growing or dying? What would you do to the facilities? What is your ideal staff size? What about programs—would you cut some, add some? What if you could have an endowment? Do you have unmet needs? Are these needs that only affect your organization and the members of your local community or do they reflect a greater national pattern? Can you contribute to improvement outside your community?

I recently attended a board retreat where we were asked to write down all the tangible things we'd want for our organization if money were not an object. We all wrote down our dreams and they were recorded on a large piece of paper that we all could see. After a few moments, the individual leading the retreat turned to us and said, "I have good news. There is not one thing on this list that you cannot have. All you have to do is either redirect current monies to these projects or encourage support from new donors for these new items."

He was absolutely right. There is nothing you cannot do with the support of the board, staff, and members of the business community. Perhaps it is a matter of redirecting monies or encouraging giving to support new programming or building. Perhaps it is targeted fundraising for the construction of a new facility or renovations to your current building. Perhaps it is a drive to better equip the organization's staff with new computers. Whatever it is, this book has been developed to help you understand the process of finding out what your organization wants and needs and deciding the best way to reach that goal.

This book is also designed to help you choose a fundraising partner. Once you begin uncovering what your organization wants and needs, you will realize that it is an expensive proposition. In my experience, nonprofit organizations that embark on a campaign on their own or use part-time counsel will typically raise modest amounts compared to their true potential. Sadly, this does not leave much for unforeseen expenses or bigger dreams. That raises the obvious question, "If you can do it on your own and raise the same amount as with part-time counsel, why would you ever pay for part-time counsel?" Perhaps having a little support is worth the money to some organizations. The rest of this book is designed to outline what a respectful and reputable fundraiser will bring to your campaign and the ways we can help make your organization all that it can be.

MAIN MESSAGE

Understand the organization that you currently are.
Envision the organization that you want to be.

CHAPTER 3

Charting Your Course:
Pre-campaign Planning

Establishing the Need:

Before you commit time and energy to a capital campaign, you will want to do your due diligence to ensure that you are making the right decision for your organization. There are two types of programs that can be conducted either sequentially or in parallel to help you decide if a campaign is the best course of action for you. These programs are complementary to one another, and I recommend that you conduct them sequentially so that you learn from each. However, some clients choose to conduct these programs simultaneously. You should work with your capital campaign consultant to determine the right way to conduct these programs for your organization or nonprofit institution.

The first of these programs is a needs assessment, and the second is a discernment program. The needs assessment is intended to gather information from the members of various organizational groups—board or directors, advisory committee, business and community leaders, etc. The discernment program allows the organization's leadership to discuss the information gathered from the various groups. It is possible to run a discernment program to gather input from the various institutional leaders, but I think it is important to ask the various organizations for their opinions rather than to speak on behalf of their constituents. You might be surprised at what some of the members have to offer. Their input is valuable and should be treated as such.

Let's talk about the needs assessment first. In general, needs assessments come in two varieties: those that are done internally and those that involve outside counsel. Internal assessments are difficult to conduct and rarely result in useful information because they tend to be presented as town hall–style meetings where everyone speaks and people often talk over each other. Nonprofit organizational issues can be contentious, and this format lends itself to confusion and discord. If a board member leads the session, it is often difficult to control things without offending someone and creating hard feelings. For these reasons, I obviously do not recommend a self-assessment. Organizations that involve outside counsel typically engage either a professional facilitator, an architect, or a fundraising consulting firm to help them determine what they need to do. Certainly, I recommend using fundraising consultants, as I feel these professionals can help develop an objective view of the project rather than focusing simply on buildings. It is often helpful to see the big picture, as it were, rather than the bricks and mortar of a project. Fundraising consultants can be helpful in that area. Whoever is chosen to serve as your consultant must have extensive experience with nonprofit campaigns in order to fully grasp the complexities of your specific situation. The objective of the assessment process is to develop a comprehensive list of current organizational needs, not simply physical building requirements. This process should include separate interviews of all existing organizational committees to determine current facility, staffing, teaching, and financial needs from each perspective. Each person interviewed will provide a unique perspective on what the institution needs. This information is valuable and may expose you to opinions and needs you were not previously aware of or that you may have overlooked. By including all members of the various organizational committees, you also begin to develop ownership of the issues that are being addressed. The key is to solicit information from each committee member. Encourage participation and make sure everyone's voice is heard.

In a recent campaign, a needs assessment was conducted by those support a massive expansion of the endowment for the institution. The finance director voiced concerns over the seemingly modest endowment and a need for a financial structure for the future of the institution. Others within the senior staff of the organization were concerned about the overall facilities and deferred maintenance issues facing the nonprofit. Others were more focused on a need for an expansion of physical properties to serve the long-term growth of the institution. From that one meeting with one group, several needs were identified: enhancement of the endowment for the future financial stability of the organization, a plan to include much-needed renovations and renewal to certain areas of the facilities, and a new proposed vision for the expansion of the facilities including a fund to purchase additional properties for future use.

In another needs assessment regarding current health and human service programs, staff, volunteers, and prospective donors were particularly concerned with and expressed the need for the development of a new IT center. A needs assessment indicated that this was a top priority for many of the participants.

This same type of meeting was conducted with a variety of groups involved with the institution. Leaders of each of the groups with various concerns then brought their lists to the discernment meeting, and a comprehensive list of needs/wants was created. The administrator, board of trustees, and larger prospective donors then identified and created a priority list of the various concerns, including all aspects of building and facility needs as well as potential changes to the programs and services.

A discernment program—the second type of needs assessment—is designed especially for the leaders of the institution. It is a process by which the leaders of various committees and organizations come together and discuss their needs and wants. During the initial needs assessment, you should have compiled a list of desires from each person you interviewed. The discernment program is when you address this list.

A meeting to discuss these issues is often best conducted off-site to minimize distractions. With the daily chaos that goes into running an organization, getting away from the organization's headquarters for this assessment is key. A retreat center, if one is available, could be very useful. The meeting is best directed by an objective consultant who will motivate everyone to think outside the box and focus on the overall vision. An outsider might also recognize common problems between organizational members that might otherwise be overlooked by those too close to the problems; an outside perspective can be invaluable in this type of situation. At the same time, the consultant should keep the participants on track to accomplish their tasks of reviewing and prioritizing all of the needs and consolidating common problems that can be addressed by a single solution. By ensuring that all participants remain focused and are not sidetracked by other issues or personal interests, an outside consultant can facilitate the most productive discernment process possible.

Members of the building and finance committees should be present at the discernment meeting to answer any immediate logistical questions; for example, should the programming and services be expanded or does the organization need to purchase new property to house an expanded staff? It is especially important for members of the finance and building committees to hear firsthand from other organization leaders the intent of their needs and wants so that nothing is lost in translation. Participants should be encouraged to be open and honest about what they see as the end game for what they want. If they believe that the esteem of the institution will be raised with additional programming, they should say so. If they believe that a new administration building for staffing is necessary to attract more interest and talent in the field, that should be stated. At the conclusion of this process, the leaders of the organization should have a comprehensive list of the needs and wants of the various committees and groups along with a list of proposed solutions.

After having completed this deceptively simple process, you will have answered the question of what you need, and you will have begun the process of developing ownership among your leaders and constituency. I say "deceptively simple" because if you have everyone participating in one of these meetings, the meeting can be overtaken by personalities or hot-button issues unless an outsider can control the session. I have seen it time and again in nonprofit fundraising discussions; the board argues against spending more money on facilities, and the staff holds out for new supplies and additional staffing support. There is very little chance that everyone involved will agree; however, that is why an outside consultant as a facilitator is necessary. The goal of this meeting is to hear every participant express their desires, unify the list of needs, and unify the purpose of the campaign to meet those needs. Avoiding confrontation is the consultant's job. Let your consultant be the bad guy, cutting off discussion that veers off topic and away from the main thrust of the effort. Do not allow a staff or board member to become a target in these meetings. It is crucial that everyone feels heard and feels his or her opinions are validated.

I cannot overemphasize the importance of conducting a thorough and comprehensive needs assessment that leads to a discernment process before beginning your capital campaign in earnest. The buy-in or ownership you gain from this process is invaluable over the course of a campaign. In my experience, nonprofit organizations that skip this step do themselves a great disservice by not laying the groundwork for the campaign. In the end, the organizational employees and other constituents do not support the campaign as strongly as they could because they do not feel that sense of ownership. It is immensely powerful to be able to go back to organizational leaders and say, "You mentioned this was a critical need." They know that they were heard, and you addressed a need they had. Doesn't it make sense that you should try to get buy-in from everyone?

Moving Forward:

Now that you know what the leaders, volunteers, and prospective donors of the institution want and need, you can extrapolate that the members of the respective committees want and need the same things because they went through the needs assessment process as well. Now it is time to start talking numbers. It can be intimidating at first, but it is important to get some idea of how much everything would cost if you did everything identified in the needs assessment and discernment. If you have decided to renovate or build, now is the time to enlist the skills of an architect to tell you if the plan is possible. You will also need to collect a list of other estimated costs, such as a new auditorium or research center, and the cost for each. At the conclusion of the process, you should have a comprehensive list that looks something like the one below, depending on your specific needs (Table 1).

Table 1

Estimated Breakdown of Costs

Deferred Maintenance Issues $15,000,000
   Foundation repair
   Plastering & painting
   Window sealing restoration
   Heating & cooling system
   Exterior & interior door refurbishment
   Roof repair
   Auditorium seat replacement
   Replace lintels & stone

Exterior Vision $17,000,000
   Construction of New Administration Building
   Main entry & arrival area
   Outdoor cafeteria seating
   Replacement of the front hall
   Flagstone replacement at front entrance
   Landscaping & parking lot repairs
   Replacement of handicapped ramp

Interior Vision $15,500,000
   New auditorium sound, lights, & stage curtain
   Stage wood refurbishing
   Renovation to dressing rooms and control booth
   Public address system
   Handicapped accessibility

Staff Training Facility Refurbishment $3,250,000

Contingency Fund/Various Expenses $2,500,000
   A construction & renovation contingency
   Retirement of construction debt
   $400,000 building & renovation fund
   Permits
   Campaign expenses

Total Proposed Vision Costs $52,750,000*

This may not be what you set as your ultimate goal. This is the list that you are going to take to the prospective large donors of the institution to provide an estimate of the overall identified needs.

A good consultant will assist in finding an architect who can develop the conceptual plans you need to see your vision become a reality. The architect should be sure to include a proposed floor plan and a layout of the property site in the plans. Rough elevated renderings should also be included. With all of this, an estimate of costs should be calculated. Remember, these are only conceptual drawings, and the cost to prepare them should be kept to a minimum. Plans often change during this time, and it would be foolish to spend a great deal of time, money, and energy on architectural drawings that will probably be altered in the coming months. These plans are just a starting point. Do not invest too much time or energy in the first draft.

I was called to consult with an organization in Virginia where the leadership had hired an architect to design a much-needed renovation and addition. The architect designed an ultramodern addition to a very traditional, historic facility. He went forward with his computer-aided designs to show the building from all angles. The cost for this service was over $250,000. When I saw the design, I didn't think it fit with the design of the current facility, and I knew we did not need all the computer-generated effects, but I was there to help test the need for the proposed renovations and new addition to the institution. At the end of the focus group meetings, 100 percent of the attendees said there was a great need for the renovation and new addition. Unsurprisingly, the same 100 percent said that the proposed addition was not what they wanted. The architect contacted me at home and told me to encourage the board members to move forward with the design, saying that when it was built, everyone would love it. I informed him that you cannot make any organization move forward with plans most resisted, and without the support of the constituency, there would be no funds with which to build. Ultimately, the institution had to hire a new architect. Despite the unnecessary $250,000 expense and a four-month break waiting for the new designs, we ultimately enjoyed a highly successful campaign.

Selecting an Architect:

Ensure that the architect you hire has done work with institutions similar to yours in the past. Some architectural firms will tell you that one building project is the same as the next; this is simply not true. The appearance and functionality of an institution can be very personal to leaders, volunteers, donors, and anyone else involved in its operation. The mission and services an institution provides in a community are a calling to many people who serve and work there; it is not simply a job. Therefore, an institution is much more than just a building. Many families have been involved in the same nonprofit for several generations; it holds an important place in their hearts. An architect needs to understand that. Architects like to fully design a project, so make sure that you are only contracting the architect for conceptual drawings of a site plan, floor plans, proposed elevated rendering, and an estimated breakdown of costs. These plans will be tested in focus group meetings, and you should anticipate changes, so the design concepts should not be complete. Consider them rough drafts that the board or other constituents should feel comfortable commenting on and suggesting changes to. In addition, the more complete the plans are, the more invested the architect may be in the design. You may get resistance from them if you want to change the design; however, it is important that the architect you hire also be responsive. While it is likely that your architect will be working on multiple projects, it should seem to you that your project is the most important one for your architect. Since there is no standard fee for architectural services, you should speak to other similar institutions in the area who have recently built or renovated their buildings to get an idea of the fees you may be charged. As with any contract you sign, read it carefully. Your consultant must be able to work with the architect and, in many cases, will refer your organization's leaders to architects that have experience with similar institutions.

> During a campaign in the Washington, DC, area, one of the leaders encouraged me to visit with the architect to ensure the renderings and other materials were going to be ready for the focus group meetings. In the hour I met with him, we discussed the current project as well as some leads I provided on several projects being considered in the community. I felt it was a pledge of good faith to help him in his career. The architect was incredibly grateful for the leads, and I thought nothing of the time I had spent with him. A few days later, the client informed me the architect charged them $500 for the hour I spent with him. Needless to say, I was upset. I have since warned clients to read the architectural contracts very carefully for hidden costs such as this.

Choosing a Development Partner:

At a project in Maryland, one of the leaders had prior "experience" in fundraising. She had spent the prior two years organizing the current building campaign. She had gathered a group of successful professionals whom she was certain could pull off a building campaign without outside help. They had met from time to time to discuss the plans, but nothing ever went beyond those meetings. I happened to call upon the group, and they informed me that they were planning to build and had been working on it for a couple years. I scheduled a meeting and explained our methods regarding fundraising and offered a written proposal. They immediately embraced our services and the organization of our campaign method. I then made a formal presentation to the board of the institution, and the only one who voted against us was the woman who had been leading the effort for two years. She was determined not to pay the fee for a consultant when she was certain they could do the project on their own if given a little more time. The individuals supporting our services were diplomatic and instrumental in explaining to the board that two years had come and gone with nothing to show for it. It was obvious that while well-meaning, the committee lacked the organization skills to take on such a project. In the end, the chair leading the floundering effort was outvoted. When the campaign raised more than anyone thought possible, she told me how happy she was to be overruled. To this day, she sends me tickets to the annual spring event, and my entire family attends.

For obvious reasons, it is difficult for me to be very objective in this chapter. I believe that the method of fundraising my firm employs not only raises more money, it also raises the spirit and cohesiveness of the community of the nonprofit client. My plan encourages unity and team building. We encourage ownership, not delegation, which is particularly important when we are talking about an institution responsible for providing a service. I can only speak about my success and where I have seen others fail. Personally, I would consider a campaign that raises only a modest amount and that encourages indebtedness to be a failure. However, many boards and administrators would consider this a success because that is what the consultant they hired told them to expect. Many other fundraisers are masters at managing the expectations of the board of an institution. They tell you what they can easily help you accomplish and no more.

Many times, I have presented our method of fundraising to the board of a prospective client following another firm's presentation. This prospective client then tells me: "We were just informed that anyone who tells us that we can raise enough to meet all of our current needs is lying." The first few times it happened, I was surprised. I knew it was possible but needed a way to prove it to potential clients. I have since documented all of our success stories. Even so, the stories are often initially met with skepticism. I always encourage a prospective client to call our references. Once they do, I tend to get a call from them telling me that they cannot believe our results. Usually I respond by saying, "Let me help you believe." We have been so successful on so many capital campaigns that using the total of their current and immediate needs is a reasonable benchmark for our clients to reach for.

Several years ago, I presented our plan of campaign to the leaders of a building project with a $16 million price tag. I told these leaders that by using our method of fundraising, they could expect to raise at least that amount. They told me that they did not believe they could raise nearly enough for the needs they had. The total cost of the new building was $16 million. I informed them that $16 million would be a wonderful achievement and convinced them that we would have to think bigger. I was a little nervous as we moved forward with this project. Very often, if leaders convince themselves they are unable to achieve a particular objective, it becomes a self-fulfilling prophecy. But the volunteers working on this campaign poured their hearts and souls into it and ignited the spirits within the community. In the end, they raised over $16 million, and again, a client learned how successful they could be with the right plan in place.

Of course, if you have a member of the board or administration who is experienced in fundraising and can devote adequate time to the campaign, you may not need outside counsel. This would be a terrific scenario for most organizations because it would keep costs low. However, there are some potentially serious pitfalls to this approach. If this individual is a volunteer and does not perform, are you going to fire him or her? How can you fire a volunteer? If the campaign is not progressing or your volunteer has a family emergency and needs to step away, who is going to take the reins? Are you willing to put the needs of the entire organization in the hands of a volunteer?

Even with the best intentions—and sometimes years of experience—a volunteer can only do so much.

Additionally, it is worth considering whether this member of the board can be truly objective regarding the organization's needs. If he or she tries to lead the board or administration members in a direction they do not agree with, will there be hard feelings? Will they balk at supporting the campaign? If the member hears things during the campaign that he or she thinks you won't like to hear, will you be told? How might you guarantee the confidentiality of the campaign records? Will this person be privy to all the pledged amounts?

Today, most nonprofit organizations have a development director or even a department dedicated to fundraising. While this person or staff may have experience in fundraising, a building project requiring many millions of dollars may be too large and complicated for them to direct alone. One of the chief responsibilities of a development director is to manage the annual giving to the institution. It may be difficult to direct both a capital campaign and the annual campaign. Much will depend on the size and experience of the staff available to the development director.

In the end, organizations that attempt a campaign on their own—no matter how good their staff and volunteers are—will usually raise modest amounts compared to the potential the organization has in the community. This is assuming the effort ever gets off the ground.

If you choose to hire outside counsel—and I highly encourage you to do so—you should select an experienced firm that will be a true partner with you on your journey. The firm must have experience in fundraising similar to the needs of your institution. The firm should work on an at-will contract, so that if for any reason the campaign is going slowly or something happens that necessitates the campaign being put on hiatus, you are not committed to paying for services when you cannot use them. The following is the story of a school that learned a very valuable but costly lesson, one that you will hopefully not have to learn yourself.

A nonprofit organization used a part-time firm to help with a major building campaign. The fundraising firm did not believe in conducting a feasibility study; instead, it encouraged the leaders and volunteers to begin the capital campaign immediately. Unfortunately, the project was not well thought out, and there was little ownership among the business and community leaders. Several weeks into the campaign effort, the decision was made to end the attempt. Unfortunately, the organization had signed a contract with the part-time firm for the entire length of the campaign. Even though the effort ended abruptly and in disaster, the firm demanded payment. Sadly, the total fee of over $250,000 still had to be paid by the institution.

In contrast, with all the hurricane activity we have experienced over the past few years, our clients in Florida, Texas, New Jersey, and other affected areas always have the option to take time off from the campaign. With an at-will contract, there was no negative consequence. When they are ready to resume the campaign, our consultant returns promptly.

If you are still reading, I will presume that you are considering using outside counsel. Congratulations! Now I will outline and explain the types of service you will have offered to you. You will have a choice of full-time consulting or part-time consulting. So how do you decide which is best for you and your organization?

First, you have to establish how much you need to raise to do all the things you need or want to do. Use the information from your needs assessments when determining this. Most part-time firms do not believe in conducting either a needs assessment or a discernment program because those types of meetings are time intensive and tie up one of their consultants. Therefore, if you go with a part-time consulting firm, you likely will not have the benefit of a consultant running your needs assessments. You could attempt to conduct it yourself.

Based on your needs assessment, if you only need to raise a modest amount compared to your fundraising potential, you could hire a part-time firm or do it yourself; the results are generally the same. However, if your needs are more significant, you would do well to hire a full-time consulting firm; that is what I would recommend. If you consider return on investment, part-time consulting could cost you up to 20 percent of the total amount you raise. In using a full-time consulting firm, your overall consulting costs decrease to approximately 2 to 4 percent. The reason for this is primarily the large amount of funds your organization can potentially raise when your campaign is directed by a full-time consultant working with all your volunteers, seven days a week.

Be very wary of any firm or individual that offers to be compensated based on a percentage of the funds pledged. This can cause a conflict of interest for the fundraiser. It may put the consultant in a position to put pressure on organizational leaders and volunteers for higher-amount gifts. The last thing you want is for your prospective donors or board members to feel pressured to make higher contributions simply because a consultant will earn more money. Encouragement to raise funds is good, but undue pressure can only harm the reputation of the organization and will stress out those working on the campaign.

> In a presentation to ask a prospective donor to consider a pledge of $200,000, the donor confessed that it would be a significant amount of her retirement and that she would be much more comfortable contributing $100,000. The volunteer and I gladly accepted the generous pledge and left. In the car on the way back to the office, the volunteer admitted that while he initially thought that it would have been an advantage to work with a firm that only worked on a percentage to motivate them to raise more money for the project, that would not have been the best thing for this woman or the reputation of the institution. He was grateful for a firm that was working on a flat fee and in the best interest of the institution.

How do you find a Capital Campaign consulting firm?

When you are searching for a capital campaign consulting firm to assist you, you have several options. You can look on the Internet and pick a few different firms to interview, or you can call around to area nonprofits and ask for recommendations. However, there is really no shortcut to making this decision. In the end, you are going to have to choose from a few recommended firms and interview them to see which method best suits your expectations. You must do your due diligence when selecting a firm, but it will pay off in the end.

During this interview process, you need to learn a few things about the firm and its consultants, decide if the consultant is a good fit with your organization, and decide if you like the approach the firm takes for capital campaigns. Remember that you can veto the consultant the firm presents to you if you do not like him or her. You have a choice. However, you should also remember that if you have identified a consultant with whom you want to work, you should move quickly, as the consultant may be assigned to another campaign if you delay.

When nonprofit organizations are faced with making a decision regarding a consulting firm, I provide them with some questions to act as guidelines. These questions are:

1. Does the firm provide full- or part-time service? When you get your answer, ask why the type of service the firm provides is superior to others. If the representatives do not think it is superior, why do they offer this type of service?

2. What is the average length of a campaign for a particular financial goal and an organization of our size? How does that compare with other institutions of other sizes? What factors drive whether a campaign is made shorter or longer?

3. Will your consultant be available to us to meet the needs of our volunteers, or will we have to arrange our volunteers around the consultant's schedule?

4. Will your service provide us with a consultant who can accompany us on personal visits and presentations to prominent board members, as well as business and community leaders? If the schedule changes at the last minute, will the consultant be flexible?

5. Do you feel that there is value to your participation in a readiness assessment/ feasibility study before the campaign, or could we do one on our own? If you can perform one, does the organization's leadership need to be involved? Would you favor conducting more personal interviews or more group meetings? How do you structure these meetings?

6. Before the readiness assessment/feasibility study, does your firm help us, or should we anticipate preparing on our own until you arrive for the first meeting?

7. What is the cost for this preliminary work provided by your firm?

8. What is the number-one reason we should choose your firm? The amount of money you raise? The impact your service has on the volunteers? The length of the campaign? The effect on our staff and volunteers?

If you have read the previous section of this book, you know that some of these are trick questions. How a firm answers them is very telling of the service it will provide during the campaign.

After learning about the different types of services offered, you must decide how much time and effort you can expect staff and volunteers at your organization to contribute to the administration of the campaign.

No matter what a consulting firm tells you—whether it offers part-time or full-time service—someone at your institution is going to be responsible for the campaign 100 percent of the time. If you have a full-time consultant, the head of your institution and members of the campaign committee will not have to be the ones drafting letters, training volunteers, picking up brochures, and contacting speakers; the consultant should be doing that work. Some part-time firms will encourage you to hire an additional person to assist in the campaign. However, what this ultimately means is that you are paying a consulting firm to instruct you to add to your staff—and increase your payroll. This is often the most expensive way to run a campaign. When you factor in the fee for the part-time firm and the salary of a new employee, hired only for their assistance in the campaign, you have already spent a great deal of money. This is particularly troubling if the campaign is only aimed at achieving a modest goal. All of a sudden, the campaign does not seem to be raising enough, and the success of the campaign comes into question.

Whomever you ultimately choose for a consulting firm, ensure that they will help you achieve the following:

During the Readiness Assessment / Feasibility Study:

1. The consultant should help you collate the data and develop an effective Case for Support.
2. The consultant should not only coach all of your focus group presenters and write the scripts, but should also attend every Focus Group Meeting and take notes on the comments during the question and answer section.
3. The consultant should also accompany you to all personal interviews.
4. The consultant should develop an effective questionnaire and tabulate the responses for his or her final report to you.
5. Finally, he or she should prepare a professional final report that you and the organizational leaders can use to discuss next steps.

It is important for the consultant to be involved in the focus group meetings so that he or she can answer questions that arise. While this is not the best time to give detailed information about a potential campaign, volunteers and prospective donors need to hear about the options of moving forward with a capital campaign based on a three-to five-year pledging period.

For the Campaign:

1. Develop a Plan of Campaign:

    The consultant should present you with job descriptions for each of the key campaign members and help to identify and recruit the right leader for each position. Since your consultant has been involved in the focus group meetings and has met many of the potential campaign leaders, he or she should be invaluable in recommending individuals to fill the important leadership roles. The consultant should provide assistance in organizing the campaign committees, and he or she should attend any session at your request. The consultant should create a campaign calendar that coordinates the activities of all committees so that, at a glance, you will be able to see what is happening with the campaign and when

2. Campaign Materials:

    All printed materials, including the view book, the visitor's handbook, and the campaign brochure are key presentation tools and should be drafted by the consultant. It is essential that the consultant put these materials together so that they are effective and concise and reflect the personality of your institution. This job should only be done by a professional. The materials must be planned carefully so that they are ready when they are needed. These materials include pledge cards, which must be designed and printed. Someone with experience is needed to oversee this process and to ensure that the pledge cards are correct and arrive on time.

3. Education and Coaching:

    A full-time consultant gives you flexibility. His or her schedule is determined by you for the duration of the campaign. The consultant can therefore conduct training sessions at convenient times for your volunteers—not only when the consultant is available. He or she can respond to changes in scheduling and can attend all meetings and make personal visits. The consultant also continually monitors the progress of the various committees and is able to foresee, warn about, or respond to potential concerns or emergencies before they become problematic. One of the consultant's primary responsibilities is to coordinate the training of all individuals who will be soliciting campaign pledges from donors. Part-time consultants struggle with all of this due to their limited availability. Often they end up assigning these tasks to someone on your staff.

4. Campaign Reports/Records:

Your consultant should provide you and other appropriate members with a weekly report on the progress of the campaign. This way, you are able to stay abreast of the campaign. The consultant will keep the pledge card report and gift records up to date and oversee the timely sending of thank-you letters to contributors. He or she will also submit a final report to you on the entire campaign effort once the campaign has concluded. This will allow you to see all phases of the campaign process and to determine what worked, what did not, and what could be improved for next time.

5. Post-Campaign Procedures:

At the end of the consultant's time with you, he or she will turn over all materials to you and your staff and continue to provide training to keep the campaign alive. For a few months after the campaign, the consultant will periodically call to check on the progress of the campaign. This service should be provided to you at no charge.

I overheard a competing part-time fundraiser talking to a nonprofit administrator about the service his firm could provide. The administrator asked, "How often is the consultant actually here at our headquarters during the campaign?" The fundraiser responded, "As often as you think you need us."

This is how most part-time firms operate, but I think it is essential that a consultant be in residence for the duration of the project. It is obviously your choice, and you are welcome to spend $5,000 a day, plus expenses, on a consultant who flies back and forth as needed, but if this is your first campaign, how will you know when you need the consultant? Often, you will not know until it is too late and you find yourself in real trouble. Aren't you hiring an experienced consultant so that he or she can tell you what is needed and anticipate any problems you might face? An on-site, full-time consultant will see the problems before they arise, saving you crucial time and money. Many of the part-time firms will tell you that they can manage your campaign in six or eight on-site visits. That does not sound so bad, but if you divide their total fee by the number of times they are physically present at your organization, you may find that you are paying $20,000 or more per visit. When you look at it that way, a part-time consultant does not seem like such a bargain.

The following chart illustrates what I see to be the differences between full-time and part-time consulting:

Resident-Directed, Full-time Consulting	Part-time Consulting
Available any time 24/7 to the volunteers and organization staff. Personal attention is given to the client in all phases of the campaign.	Time is divided among multiple clients. As many as eight to ten projects at once. No client enjoys exclusive personal attention.
Campaign is of shorter duration. Volunteers remain enthusiastic and committed.	Usually several months longer in duration. Lengthy campaigns can overburden and exhaust staff and volunteers.
Campaign potential is significantly greater. Firm can attend all personal visits to prospective donors.	Limited potential. Director usually unable to participate in personal visits.
On-site and available to monitor and address all campaign issues as they arise.	Off-site and not available to identify potential concerns which arise. Unable to address unanticipated concerns immediately.
Personally observes campaign progress and determines where professional experience is needed.	Relies on volunteers to identify areas that need attention.
Available when volunteers require coaching. All meetings occur at convenience of volunteers.	Training and meeting times are subject to the availability of the part-time Director. Schedule must compete with other campaigns the firm is directing.
Prepares all campaign materials for client approval.	Staff, board members, and volunteers must complete all campaign work.
Director totally involved in the life of the organization and staff meetings. Participates in all aspects of the Capital Campaign and available to visit prospective donors.	Usually not available to participate in visits with prospective donors or staff meetings. Director usually only available over telephone or through email between visits.
Fees and expenses are predictable and controlled.	In addition to campaign fees and expenses, nonprofit client is usually responsible for additional items such as airfare, hotel, auto rental, telephone calls and meals.

I was the second of two firms to present to a nonprofit board in Indiana. After I finished my presentation, the board president thanked me. I asked about the other firm that presented and the president rolled her eyes. She said that the consultant came into the meeting flustered and frustrated because his plane had been delayed. He then went on to complain that he was exhausted from running between the ten campaigns he was currently directing. The president informed me that our approach of having one consultant focused on one campaign was a welcome prospect and a relief. We made a positive impression on the board president and were given the opportunity to direct what turned out to be a very successful campaign.

After you interview a number of consulting firms, you will need to choose one based on the responses to your plans and personalities. Regardless of time, money, and dedication to the campaign, you must also go with your intuition. Does the consulting firm address your organization's needs in a way that feels genuine and caring? Does the potential consultant do more than is asked, or does he or she meet the minimum requirements without showing initiative? Does the consultant truly support the mission of your nonprofit organization? Many people will feel many different ways about the potential consulting firm. There may be strong opinions within the organization's leadership; there will not always be a consensus. You need to allow everyone to voice his or her opinions and concerns and then vote.

Many firms claim that if you keep the organization's mission at the forefront, the right firm will find you. However, I firmly believe that the harder you work, the luckier you become. You must do your due diligence when selecting a firm. My firm provides teaching in practical development growth skills to the staff and volunteers involved in the campaign. Their mission is to then use those skills to teach others. As service providers, we have a deep sense of obligation to our organization and our community, and teaching development skills that can be used to raise funds for the improvement of our nonprofits is as important as any other part of the educational process.

The last thing I want you to remember is the campaign committee. While it is too early to select the members of the campaign at this stage, you can start thinking about it. You will most likely have people jockeying for the positions while others try to distance themselves from the responsibility. It may be tempting to promise the positions to those who want them to feel as though you have taken some important steps in beginning your campaign. Nevertheless, at this point, you must resist that temptation.

Allow your experienced consultant to help you identify leaders through the step we will discuss in Chapter 5, the readiness assessment/feasibility study. If you work with your consultant and truly assess the strengths and weaknesses of those potential committee members, you will find the right people for the roles.

MAIN MESSAGE

Even if you have been involved in a campaign in the past, you need a qualified, dedicated partner to work with you throughout this process. Choose your partner carefully and make sure that you fully understand the service you will be provided. Discounted prices tend to reflect discounted service. Very seldom is the cheapest product the best. Let a professional help your organization's leaders compile a list of their needs and wants; then let him or her help the leadership package their vision and test it in a feasibility study.

CHAPTER 4
Crucial Elements of a Successful Campaign: The Four Main Ingredients

When we discuss fundraising for nonprofit organizations, we use the word *development*. However, a synonym for *development* is *stewardship*, which comes from the word *steward*, meaning custodian or keeper. So we must ask ourselves: What are we in custody of? What are we keeping? When we talk about nonprofits, we are responsible for service to our community. We must be the custodians of our organization's mission. Therefore, it is reasonable to say that a fundraising campaign is a way of keeping or growing our work in the nonprofit sector. However, as time goes by, we have come to equate fundraising and development with the financial aspects of nonprofit projects, as we learn quickly that those things we need or want for our organizations require more funding. While money and fundraising are necessarily the focus of most nonprofit development campaigns, we must not lose sight of the other important parts of the campaign. A development campaign is an opportunity to grow the facilities; to enhance the programming; to elicit the input of board members, administrators, staff, and members; and to decrease debt. In a successful capital campaign, it is important to include everyone who considers themselves part of your nonprofit organization's community. It is not enough to simply involve those individuals whom we perceive as wealthy. Far too many campaigns focus on those whom its organizers feel can make large contributions and pass over the average prospective donor. Not only does this irritate the past large donors, but it leaves a great amount of potential money unsolicited. Remember, whether a campaign has a goal of $5 million, $10 million, or considerably more, all contributions are needed in order for the campaign to be successful. A sure way to eliminate potential major funds and alienate volunteers as a whole is to not include them in the campaign process. When this happens, those same volunteers search for other institutions to offer their support. All pledges are important in a capital campaign. Not everyone should be expected to give the same amount, but they should be given the same consideration for their gift based on their ability. Important initiatives at the organization are funded by the generosity of the financial supporters of the institution. It is an essential part of any campaign to find out what your organization's community wants to support. It is also important to educate the community about what you already support. Make sure that your organization is proud of what it has accomplished. If your organization has produced a great number of award winners, now is the time to mention it. If your staff has received special recognition for outstanding work, that should be trumpeted. If one of your programs has been critically reviewed, you would want to talk about that as well. It is important that potential donors understand that even without the campaign, your organization is doing great things. Imagine what you could do with more funding! We cannot be passive about needed funding for important initiatives. We must be bold and proud to serve and support the work of the organization.

The highest levels of your organization's leadership must have the firm conviction that the decision to conduct this campaign has evolved out of the vision, work, mission, ideals, and planning of the organization's supporters and is dedicated to the advancement of the organization's mission. Those in charge must firmly believe in the necessity of the campaign and have a fervent desire to improve their organization. The basic aim of the campaign is to go beyond fundraising. Raising money is all well and good, but it is not enough. Particularly in an economy where nonprofit service organizations receive less attention than in the past, a successful campaign broadens the community's commitment to service, develops new nonprofit leaders, and fosters a sense of community and pride, in addition to raising money.

There are four main ingredients to a successful capital campaign. The four ingredients overlap, and eventually, blend together. However, no one ingredient is more important than the others; they are all essential to success.

The first component of a successful Capital Campaign is the **Case Statement**. It is the clear, concise reason that your community should support the campaign. The case statement is developed after you have been through all of the meetings with all of the individual groups—board, financial supporters, staff, members, etc.—and met with your organization's leadership to discuss all of the reasons a campaign is necessary. This is the time for your nonprofit leaders to lead the discussion and the process. This is also the time when difficult decisions must be made. Many people will have questions, and you will need to be ready to explain why certain courses of action were chosen over others. If you have chosen to focus on raising funds for a theater space instead of expanding office space for your staff, be prepared to explain why. If you have decided to raise money to replace the roof of your organization's headquarters instead of re-surfacing the sports court, you need to be able to justify this decision. Whether you have decided to acquire property, to renovate, to build, or to pay off debt, this is the time for you to make your decisions clear and understandable to your organization's members and constituency. In addition to the proposed floor plans, property site plan, and a good estimate of costs, it is important to include how current service models will be enhanced or how new models will be implemented. If you are planning a complete overhaul of part of your organization, you must explain how that will happen. Far too often, the focus is on the brick-and-mortar aspect of the project; service should be the motivating concern. While it is easier to put dollar amounts on renovation projects or purchasing of physical items (e.g., computers or sports equipment), it is important to remember that the greater goal of the campaign is to improve the experience for staff and your organization's members.

The second ingredient you must have while conducting your Capital Campaign is **Leadership**. Although you have chosen a course of action as a group, this is the time when someone must lead the group to consensus. You must ensure that all of your leaders are on the same page when it comes to understanding and agreeing on the most urgent needs of your organization and the solutions you have identified. It is important that members of the board, staff, administration, and potential large donors are involved. In addition, the building and finance committees must support and be involved with the project. There will always be people who do not agree with your methods or your plans. You will probably have staff and volunteers who will tell you that they think the capital campaign is a mistake. These are often people who feel overtaxed as it is and who are concerned about committing extra time and energy to a campaign. They might be staff members who are overworked and underpaid or volunteers who feel that they already give all they can to the organization. They may feel that they simply do not have enough time to dedicate to the campaign. You need to convince them that there is enough evidence that changes are wanted by the organization and that such changes will help them in the end. Assure them that you will test the plan with the organization's constituency before moving forward. You will not implement any changes without first checking for feasibility with the organization. Convince the skeptics to at least allow the constituency to hear the plan. If they refuse, allow them the opportunity to graciously step down from their positions. This can be difficult when dealing with staff and members, but you can suggest to them that they refrain from participating in any campaign activities if they have strong objections. In every campaign, there are people who will never be won over and who will serve as a constant thorn in your side throughout. It is best to deal with them early and decisively and to move on as swiftly as possible.

In these early meetings, you will be tempted to try to name the campaign chair, or other leaders of the campaign. It will seem ideal to have someone in place as you begin the campaign in earnest. However, you must resist that temptation. Your campaign consultant will be able to help you identify the right campaign chair. He or she is more experienced and will help you find the person who will best support the mission and reach the desired outcome of the campaign. Additionally, it is the campaign consultant who will ultimately pledge his/her support to the chair to let him or her know that the consultant will do the bulk of the work. It is important that the campaign consultant and the campaign chair have a good working relationship built on mutual respect and a shared vision.

The third essential ingredient in your campaign is your **Constituency**. You need to engage all members of the organization's constituency, not just the board members or administration. Even if you have constituents who do not frequently participate in your organization's activities, functions, or initiatives, you must include them. Everyone's experience with the nonprofit is important. Once you have established an exhaustive list of your constituency, you will need to send a letter to everyone announcing the focus group meetings (discussed in the next chapter). Your consultant should develop the letter for you with your approval. The goal of this letter is to send out a teaser message, a preview of coming attractions, if you will. A common mistake made by nonprofit organizations conducting their own campaigns is to send out an initial letter that outlines the entire plan for the campaign. If you provide too much information in this first letter, your constituency may feel that they already know all the information they need to know, and therefore, they will be less likely to welcome a personal interview or attend a focus group meeting to learn more.

When constructing your teaser message, your campaign consultant should consider the inclusive nature of the message. It should read something like: "Our board members and other volunteers have been working on immediate and long-range plans and are now ready to present those plans for discussion. The opinions of the community are important." Many administrators boldly declare that all supporters will have an opportunity to meet with the organization's leaders to discuss the future plans. Others want to include only those leaders who are most active in the community, such as the development committee and administration. Although many organizations tend not to want to conduct campaigns during the summer, as people tend to travel and business is more relaxed, waiting until the fall to begin the campaign is often problematic because people very quickly get busy in school and work activities and have less time to devote to meetings and planning sessions. Most of the time, it only slows down your timing to wait until the fall to begin your campaign. However, as the following story illustrates, there is merit in visiting personally with members during the slow season.

In a recent campaign, one of the most dedicated families lived in the community only during the school year. The rest of the time, they were farther north, where they had lived most of their lives and where their extended family now lived. The organization administrator waited to meet with them personally to explain the building project and campaign plans in detail. Most leaders of the campaign were skeptical of any meaningful involvement, since the family was not present in the community for the duration of the year. Nevertheless, even though they were only part-time residents of the town, the family was happy to meet with the administrator and ultimately contributed significantly to the campaign. Their involvement and giving was instrumental to the success of this project.

The final ingredient necessary for a successful Capital Campaign is the **Plan of Campaign.** This is a process implemented by an experienced consultant. This is the core reason why it is valuable to employ a full-time firm to plan your campaign. Your plan of campaign must be a well-tested and proven plan that begins by soliciting your constituents for input and then engaging them step by step through the process of the campaign.

Another important item to keep in mind is the timing of each aspect of the campaign. Frequently, I am asked, "When should we conduct our campaign?" Understandably, organizations are anxious to begin raising funds as soon as possible. Being mindful of that, I usually reply, "Right after we finish a thorough feasibility study." While most nonprofit leaders believe that a fall campaign is best because it sets the tone for the next fiscal year, the fact is that the best time to conduct your capital campaign is when you and the other organizational leaders are prepared to make the campaign your top priority for several months.

There are cases where, depending on the climate in your area, waiting for better weather may be a prudent idea. Maine in the winter and Louisiana in the summer may be difficult times for campaigns. In addition to their normal concerns and schedules, your constituency are likely to be dealing with weather-related challenges—and often unforeseen financial challenges—leaving them less time to dedicate to the campaign. However, there is no hard and fast rule regarding climate and the timing of campaigns. I have personally directed projects in every area of the country during every season, and those campaigns have yielded great results. This is another reason why a seasoned consultant is beneficial. He or she will have experience with these types of issues and will be able to draw on that experience to best plan the timing of your campaign.

My larger point is that every organization and every town is different. It is less important to make a decision based on the calendar than it is to determine the availability of the organization's leaders and the community as a whole. In the next chapter, we will discuss the ways in which we determine whether these four ingredients are in place and if you should move forward with a campaign or return to the drawing board to start again.

MAIN MESSAGE

There are four ingredients to make a successful campaign: Case Statement, Leadership, Constituency and a Plan of Campaign. All elements must be present and in place in order to proceed.

CHAPTER 5

Readiness Assessment / Feasibility Study: Engaging Your Leaders and Constituency

Recently, I spoke with the development director of a large nonprofit organization. During our talk, he told me that they were focused on raising $20 million for a particular building project. I explained to the development director that the need should be tested with a thorough feasibility study that would engage members of their constituency and share the vision of the institution. He thanked me for my input and then told me that there was no need for a feasibility study because they had already identified the needs for the campaign and they had decided that any money raised would go solely toward what the board and staff felt was important. I asked him why he believed that people would donate to a cause if they had no voice in determining it. "People will give because it is the right thing to do," he said emphatically. I wished him the best of luck, but knew in my heart that the campaign was going to be a disaster for them. As I predicted, a few months later, they abandoned the campaign. While I am certain that the development director genuinely believed that he was doing the best thing for his organization, his arrogance misled him.

There is no place for arrogance in nonprofit fundraising. Enlisting the help of a professional consultant does not mean that you are not capable of addressing your organization's needs and the desires of your constituents. It means that you care enough about doing this right that you want to make sure you give yourself every opportunity to conduct the best campaign possible.

A readiness assessment, which is sometimes called a feasibility study, is an essential part of the campaign process. The main purpose of this study is to put the plan decided on by the organization's leaders in front of the constituency to test it. This is not the time to open the floor for new ideas and proposals, although it is important to be respectful to those who wish to weigh in. Instead, the objective is exactly as is stated: to test the feasibility of the proposed campaign. This is your opportunity to take your proposed plan back to your constituency and to ask them, "Will this proposed campaign meet our immediate needs?" In addition, the time to do it is now, before you begin your campaign in earnest.

The first objective of the study is to determine whether the constituency agrees with the leadership's assessment of the state of the organization's facilities, programs, activities, etc. As is sometimes the case, leadership spends a great deal of time discussing the potential needs of the campaign and can often have a difficult time constructing an unbiased or outside view of the situation. This is the opportunity for the rest of the constituency to point out to the leadership something that might have been missed. Likewise, it is also an opportunity for the members to tell the leadership if they have misjudged the importance of a component of the campaign. Being too close to the campaign can be a handicap for some leaders; this is when they are able to gain a different perspective.

The second objective of the process allows the organization's supporters to identify strengths and weaknesses in the case. Through this process, the prospective donors can help prioritize what they identify as the most important needs of the campaign. For example, the leadership of a theater nonprofit—having been influenced by the arts director—may have determined that a new auditorium is needed. The constituency could point out that, in fact, only the seating needs to be replaced and the remainder of the funds can go toward renovating the staff offices, which are crumbling and outdated.

Third, differing viewpoints can be heard about current organizational needs and programs. This is an opportunity to allow supporters to voice concerns and to provide the leaders with a chance to respond. It can be a very useful part of the process. Often, people want to feel as though they are part of the process, and allowing them to voice their opinions in this environment makes them feel heard and acknowledged. It is crucial that everyone be allowed to speak. Often, people will discover that what they thought were differences of opinion were merely a result of miscommunication and can be cleared up before things get too far.

The process also has some secondary objectives, including developing ownership of the ideas among the constituency, discovering new leaders, and creating excitement for the campaign and support for the organization's leaders.

> During a feasibility study for a nonprofit campaign in California, the leadership was testing support from the supporters of the organization for both a new heating and cooling system and the purchase of some property across the street for a new parking lot. Neither of these items was especially exciting to the organization's supporters. However, during one of the focus group meetings, the athletic director stated that if he had his way, there would be new training and exercise equipment. This electrified the supporters. The equipment was added to the case along with the heating and cooling system and the parking lot. With the exercise equipment at the forefront, the campaign raised enough funds to pay for all the equipment, the heating and cooling system, the parking lot, and the creation of an endowment. If I am being honest, I truly believe that everyone who donated was considering the exercise equipment when they donated because it was, by far, the most exciting part of the campaign.

Some fundraising consulting firms will offer to conduct personal interviews with your most affluent constituents on their own. They will offer to take this off your plate, claiming that they do not want to "waste your time" with this preliminary business. They may also tell you that if a staff or board member is present for the interview, the individuals interviewed will not offer up an honest assessment of their opinions. This is entirely false. The fact is, a readiness assessment, or feasibility study, should be used to assist in convincing prospective donors that there is a significant need that must be addressed. It is an opportunity to presell a campaign effort and to enlist support from your supporters. A hired consultant with no prior relationship to the individual being interviewed cannot be expected to help lay the groundwork necessary for a successful campaign effort. He or she will not understand the ins and outs of the organization and cannot fully grasp the desires of the organization's members. You run the risk of sending the wrong message to members of the community if you send a hired consultant to take the place of a fellow supporter. When this occurs, I always recommend that organization's leaders accompany the consultant to conduct interviews and do not send consultants alone to do it for them. Even though it seems appealing, and you will likely relish the opportunity to have some things taken off your plate, if you or a board member is not conducting the interviews, how will you know if the consultant is asking the right questions? How will you know how many people they are interviewing? Moreover, how do you know that what they are reporting back to you is an accurate assessment of what was said? Of course, it is in the best interest of the consultant to put a positive spin on the comments or to sugarcoat their reports to you; they want you to proceed with a campaign and continue to pay their consulting fee. This is precisely the reason why it is important for organizational leaders to accompany consultants on all interviews. The entire campaign process is a team effort, and by presenting a united front to your constituents, it will be seen that way.

Recently, my firm was called by an organization to conduct a feasibility study and capital campaign. A few months before they contacted us, the organization had contracted with a part-time fundraising firm to conduct their version of a feasibility study. The members of the board liked the idea of allowing this firm to conduct all the personal interviews themselves without involving the members or leadership. The organization believed that the firm would target a large portion of the influential and affluent members of the community for interviews. Several months passed, and the organization received a bill for $25,000 from the part-time firm. The board members were presented with the findings of the seventeen personal interviews the consulting firm had conducted. The board members were shocked that so few interviews had been conducted and that people of influence and affluence were not well represented among those interviewed. The findings were sketchy at best—sketchy and expensive! However, despite the unimpressive results, the firm went ahead with recommending a major capital campaign. When they received this recommendation, many board members asked, "How can you recommend such an aggressive campaign when you didn't even meet with the community's most wealthy andand influential leaders?"

The consultant's answer was that they were not able to schedule meetings with those people because they were "unwilling to schedule time with us."

This should not have been a surprise because people do not generally want to meet with people they do not know. They viewed these fundraisers as hired guns, doing work the organization's leaders should have been doing.

During my initial meeting with the organization's leadership, I informed the board that while we generally do not like to come into a problematic situation and try to fix it, the good news was that little damage had been done as a result of so few meetings having been conducted. My firm stepped in and assisted the board with a genuine feasibility study, which led to remarkable results. Only after this flawed attempt did the leaders of this organization understand how vital their role was in preselling the campaign and helping to create ownership of the proposed building project.

When you conduct personal interviews and focus group meetings, the leaders of the organization must be present. The consultant plays a major role and should absolutely help out, but the leaders need to hear what their constituency is saying. In addition, an outside consultant has likely not been part of the organization or the community for a long time and cannot deliver the message of the leadership the way that someone with a personal stake in the success of the organization can. If you are not involved, it sends a clear message that the nonprofit leaders are not devoting time to this process. As a result, your organization's supporters are likely to put less time into considering their commitment to the campaign effort. Make sure you are sending the right message to your constituency.

My firm was in the running for two campaigns in the same metropolitan area. One organization was located on the outskirts of the city and the other was located downtown. Both were similar-sized institutions, with approximately the same number of constituents, and both had needs of about $6 million. I interviewed with both organizations, and at both interviews, I explained my method of focus group meetings and personal interviews and told the organizational leaders that if they conducted the campaign properly, they could raise $6 million. The board president of the downtown organization was intrigued, but he was concerned by the amount of work my plan involved. The leader of the suburban organization embraced my plan and hired my firm to conduct the organization's capital campaign. The downtown location hired a part-time firm to conduct their campaign. That firm's representative told the board that there was no need for him to be directly involved in the early stages of the campaign. The part-time representative also told the board that he would be able to predict what the organization could hope to raise by the end of the feasibility study. The part-time firm drafted a letter to the community that outlined the plan and asked for feedback. In the letter, the consultant asked how much money community members would contribute to the campaign. According to the firm, only about 30 percent of the letters were returned, and the consultant told the board that the campaign would only be able to raise $1 million. Because of this low response rate, the board felt they had no support from the community and elected not to conduct the campaign. In contrast, the suburban organization that contracted with my firm to conduct their campaign raised $6.5 million following my plan.

The failure and success of the two campaigns lay in the execution of the feasibility study. One consisted of sending an impersonal letter that was not well received. The form letter did not help to create a sense of ownership or excitement among the organization and community members. Additionally, the part-time consultant made the fatal mistake in a feasibility study; he asked what the respondents would give. I never understand why people ask this question. How can you possibly ask someone what he or she will give when you cannot even explain what the final project is going to be? Essentially, you are asking someone, "How much would you give for this future, unspecified project?" How can anyone be expected to answer that accurately? If asked up front, without a solid, tested plan, most people will give a token amount, and once they write an amount down, they are unlikely to change it. This is why these part-time firms can predict what will be donated to a campaign within a few dollars. The part-time consultant working with the downtown organization was most likely right when he said that the campaign would raise only $1 million. However, that does not make it acceptable for the organization. This is why part-time firms that ask this question of the constituents upfront get such poor results.

I was asked to come and present my plan of campaign to a nonprofit. While I was there, they shared with me the results of the last campaign they had conducted. For the previous campaign, the organization had used a part-time firm and had raised a very modest amount. I spoke about our plan of campaign and specifically about how our feasibility studies are conducted. Immediately following my presentation, one of the leaders admitted that, based on my presentation, the organization had made two fatal mistakes in the previous campaign. The first was that the focus group meetings were not open to the entire community—only select participants and constituents were included. This created a sense of exclusion. The second mistake they made was that following these initial meetings, the consultant insisted on asking everyone what they would pledge to the campaign. This generated token amounts and predicted the failure of the campaign.

As I have said before, there are two ways to approach the nonprofit community. One is through focus group meetings, and the other is through personal interviews. Focus group meetings are a good method and should be used to engage the majority of the constituency. This is the best way to get everyone together in one place and to get everything out in the open. Personal interviews are important in nonprofit development campaigns. Interviews are the best way to sell the needs of the organization to large potential supporters. However, they can also be very useful for supporters and volunteers who are unwilling to attend a group session or whose schedules won't accommodate one. There are sometimes people who feel uncomfortable speaking in front of a large group of people. Personal interviews are an effective way to connect with these members of the constituency. Personal interviews can also be reserved for supporters or volunteers who are especially against any change in the organization. Most leaders will know who they are. Instead of inviting them to participate in a forum where they have the opportunity to sour the community with their opinions, it is often better to meet with them privately. I know that conducting meetings involving someone who will monopolize the meeting for his or her own agenda is not helpful to the process. Even so, it is critical that you do not let your consultant conduct these meetings without you. They are an important way for you to hear what your constituency has to say about your proposed plan. You will probably learn something!

During a campaign I conducted in the South, I had scheduled a meeting with a prominent business leader in his office because he did not have the time to attend one of the focus group meetings. The plan was for me to meet up with the campaign chairman, and together we would call on this affluent and influential member to present the case for the campaign and to get his reaction. I arrived early and waited twenty minutes. The time for the meeting drew near, and the campaign chairman still had not arrived. I asked the businessman's secretary if I could reschedule the meeting, and she informed me that her boss was going out of town for a few weeks and would be unable to reschedule. This was a time before cell phones, so I was unable to call the campaign chair to ask about his whereabouts. Without any other options, I broke my own rule and met with this individual on my own. As I feared, he told me nothing about what he truly felt about the campaign. He was courteous and polite, but I could tell that the meeting felt like an inconvenience for him and that he did not know me, so he was unwilling to give his true opinions on the campaign.

Later that day, when I met with the campaign chair, he admitted to forgetting about the meeting. When I told him that I learned nothing from this individual and felt that he might not even support the campaign, the campaign chair was surprised. He knew this man had strong opinions about the organization and believed that he would have shared those opinions in the meeting. I told the chairman that he probably could have elicited that information had he attended the meeting with me, but I certainly was not able to do so on my own. It was a terrible missed opportunity for the campaign.

Length of the Study

The length of the study will vary depending on the amount a proposed campaign needs to raise, as well as the size of the constituency. The more people you need to interview, the more focus group meetings you need to schedule, and the longer period of time you will need to plan for in this effort.

When you conduct focus group meetings, you want to ensure that all prospective donors and volunteers are invited and have been given the opportunity to attend, even if they do not take advantage of it. You cannot force people to attend the focus group meetings, obviously, but ideally you should have twenty-five to forty members attend each meeting. The time frames and typical number of meetings vary. You can conduct anywhere from twelve meetings over four weeks to twenty-plus meetings over eight weeks, depending on the size of your constituency and prospective donors.

Who should present at the meeting?

During the focus group meeting, a variety of people can present. This is an excellent opportunity to identify potential new leaders and those who will become a crucial part of the campaign. Certainly, a board member, volunteer, or administrator should open the meeting and explain the purpose. However, it is fine for a concerned and articulate member of the nonprofit community to make the presentation to the group at large. Your consultant should work with the presenter in advance of the meeting to ensure that there is a plan for the presentation. If you have a rising star on the board or someone who is especially well liked by all members of the constituency, you should include this person as well. Likewise, if you have a staff member who has shown great interest in the project, that person is another good resource to include in the meeting. People from the building or finance committees are typically safe choices because they are intimately familiar with why the case decisions were made. If you are proposing a building campaign, including the architect can be very helpful when it is time to present the renderings. The key to the meeting is that the presenters are well prepared and practiced. The community needs to know that the leaders have the organization's best interests in mind.

In one campaign I conducted, there was a lawyer who had been instrumental in recruiting our firm to consult on the campaign and was essential in recruiting the presenters for the focus group meetings. Prior to the meeting, he decided that it was not necessary for him to practice before presenting to the group. He thought that since he was a lawyer and gave presentations for a living, he would be able to do it without any problem. Despite our encouragement that he take some time to practice, he refused to do so. Unsurprisingly, when the time for his presentation came, he stood before the group and fumbled his way through a disjointed presentation. During the question-and-answer session, he stammered through his answers, even to common questions we had anticipated. Once the presentation ended, he sat down next to me, dejected. "You were right," he said. "I should have practiced."

When you are preparing for your presentation, a schedule can be helpful. Approximately one to two weeks prior to the dry run of the presentation, scripts should be distributed to the six or eight potential presenters. You should identify two of them to present at the practice presentation, but everyone should practice on their own so they can help critique the two people who will present. It is also beneficial to invite a few key organizational leaders to the practice presentation so that they can help formulate answers to potential questions the presenters might find difficult.

You will need to conduct two presentations. The first should consist of a brief history of the organization and its place in the community. This presentation is designed for the newest members of the nonprofit community. You want to bring them up to speed and get them on the same page. This first presentation should include the organization's age, when and why it was founded, and the successes of the organization and its constituency . The presentation should conclude with a summary of the organization's current needs.

The second presentation should explain how the campaign plans to address these stated needs. These are the proposed solutions brought forth through the organization's leadership. If a building project is part of the proposed plan, this is the time to present the floor plans and rendering of any new buildings.

The agenda of the meeting should roughly follow the outline below.

- Welcome
- Opening Remarks
- History of the Organization
- Long-range Planning Process
- Conceptual Master Plan
- Question and Answer/Comment Session
- Questionnaire Completion
- Adjournment

In a recent nonprofit campaign, one of the presenters decided that he did not want to proceed according to the agenda. Instead, he wanted to open the meeting to suggestions from the organization's members and community. He told me that he liked my ideas, but he thought that more direct input from the community was needed. Since I have done this for many years and have seen it done in many ways, I told him that there were three main reasons for following the agenda:

- If you just open the meeting up for discussion straight away, it will appear that the leadership has not yet put any real thought into the needs of the organization.
- Moving straight to discussion will defeat the purpose of the Feasibility Study, which is to test the plan that the leadership is proposing.
- If people begin making new suggestions that in the end you do not incorporate, it will appear that you did not listen to or value their ideas.

I reminded the presenter that this was a focus group meeting and not a town hall meeting. Our purpose was to test the plans and vision that the organization's leaders had decided upon, not to solicit new ideas. I pointed out that if the prospective donors did not agree with the proposed plans, they would make it known, and it could create problems moving forward. He relented and conducted the Feasibility Study according to the agenda with great success.

Feedback is important, which is why, toward the end of the meeting, there is time allotted for the completion of a short, pertinent questionnaire. Members should complete the questionnaire before they leave the meeting and hand in their results so that they can be read and considered immediately. Below are some sample questions to include on the questionnaire:

1.   In your opinion, what is the **most important** benefit to be realized as a result of the proposed building program for our organization?

2.   How would this building program help fulfill our organization's mission and support our members and community?

3.   Have we forgotten anything? Would you add anything to proposed plans?

4.   A Capital Campaign requires many volunteers with varying responsibilities for its successful completion. Would you consider supporting a Capital Campaign?
     Financially? YES_____ NO_____ Need more information_____
     Volunteer time? YES_____ NO_____ Need more information_____

5.   Who would you suggest for leadership roles to ensure the success of a Capital Campaign?

6.   My hope for the organization is:

7.   Do you have any additional comments regarding the proposed building program?

Notice that the third question fulfills the town hall meeting issue and allows someone to interject a new idea that was not previously presented. It also allows those who do not like to speak up in groups to have input and gives everyone an opportunity to weigh in on the proposed plan. Please notice that most importantly, nowhere in this process are people asked how much they will pledge to the campaign. This is important because these are still preliminary plans that are subject to change based on the outcomes of your meetings. When you ask for pledges, you should be asking everyone based on the same plans, and if you ask too early, your plans are bound to evolve and change before you have completed your meetings. If you ask too early, the gifts will be spontaneous and will likely be token amounts. In addition, prospective donors are unlikely to change these amounts once they have been stated. Until the right person is asking in the right way with the right materials, you should not expect more than token contributions.

One of the nonprofit leaders of a campaign on which I was working was vacationing at the beach and bumped into one of the more affluent members of the community. The affluent member had participated in the feasibility study and was very supportive of the campaign ideas. He had calculated that to meet the organization's projected needs, every prospective donor would have to pledge $25,000. This affluent supporter confided to the organization's leader that he felt particularly blessed and was going to pledge $35,000 to the campaign. When the leader returned from his vacation, he reported the information to the organization's head and to me. With the case firmly established after the final feasibility study meeting was complete, the organization's head and I visited this prospective donor with hopes of his considering a $1 million pledge, which was required for this campaign to be successful. With our view book in hand and the organization's head having practiced the case presentation, the affluent member did indeed decide to pledge $1 million. Afterwards, he told us that he had only planned on pledging $35,000 and that if he had been asked for his pledge during the feasibility study, he would have only pledged the $35,000. Nevertheless, since he had seen the process of the feasibility study and had the final case presented in a comprehensive and concise manner that made sense to him and seemed to be a good plan for the organization, he was happy to make one of the lead gifts. We were happy to have his pledge, and it was a terrific start to the campaign.

Where and when are the Focus Group Meetings?

The Focus Group Meeting does not just happen by itself. It takes a great deal of preparation and organizational leader involvement. Lining up a venue is the first challenge.

In a nonprofit campaign, one of the leaders wanted to host a focus group meeting at her home. Even though we wanted the meetings to be held at the organization's headquarters to ensure that everyone felt an equal opportunity to attend, she insisted. She created a large invitation list and hired caterers. Since she was planning the event without any input from the consultant, she neglected to secure parking in her downtown community. On the day of the meeting, after only four cars could park in her two-car driveway (no other parking was available), the other invited members abandoned the event.

These logistics are important to consider when planning these meetings. An experienced consultant is responsible for considering these issues and is tasked with bringing these questions to light ahead of time. Your consultant should foresee any potential logistical problems and address them before they become truly problematic.

I have found that these meetings can draw better attendance if they are held at the organization's headquarters following meetings, new staff member orientation, sporting events, or theater productions. People are already there and therefore do not have to plan additional trips for the meeting. There is also the potential added benefit of them being energized by an exciting performance or a satisfying athletic victory.

You should schedule as many meetings as possible within the weeks of the study. Try to secure the same space for the entire duration of the study so there is no confusion. Your presenters, consultants, and supporters will always know where the next meeting will be. Although many of the meetings can be held in conjunction with an event already scheduled, you should also schedule additional meetings in the middle of each week during the evening to be convenient for some supporters so they might have an opportunity to attend.

Before you schedule the meetings, you will need to identify a few organizational leaders who will serve as hosts for the meetings. They will be responsible for greeting attendees, making sure that attendees sign in, and ushering members to the front of the room so they have a better view of the proceedings and proposed plans. The hosts also serve to increase the feeling of ownership. The more people who are involved, the more it appears that people care about the organization and the campaign. The hosts will also be able to answer some general questions about what is going to happen at the meeting. They should tell the attendees that the meeting will take approximately one hour and explain who will be presenting. They should also let attendees know that there will be a question-and-answer period and a short survey at the conclusion of the meeting. It is also helpful for the hosts to put the attendees' minds at ease by saying something like, "This meeting is informational and educational. No one is going to ask you for money tonight."

It is the host's job to call the meeting to order and to thank everyone for attending. The host will then introduce the first presenter. Toward the end of the meeting, the host should assist in distributing the questionnaires and pens, and then help to collect them. He or she should thank everyone for attending and for their participation in the meeting and the campaign feedback process.

Prior to the meeting, you should have the proposed floor plans and renderings ready so that the presenters or the architect can practice and become familiar with the design. They should be comfortable with walking the attendees through the plans. The rendering should be dry mounted and placed on easels. While it may seem counterintuitive not to use a computer presentation method, there are two reasons why we typically do not do this. The first is that with a large printed hard copy of the plans, it is easier for multiple people to approach the plans and view them at the same time. The second reason is that while we wish it were otherwise, computer glitches are common. If the plans are presented in hard copy, the meeting can proceed even if there is a technology problem.

You might be thinking that volunteers are doing the majority of the work up to this point and you are wondering what the consultant is doing during this time. But it is important to remember that the consultant got you organized, and that he or she will be spending the meeting taking copious notes about what people are saying. He or she will collect all of the questionnaires and tabulate the results before delivering you an unbiased synopsis of what happened during the various meetings. Included in the verbal and written report will be an assessment of the support the consultant feels you either have or do not have for your campaign. Your consultant will also provide you with a list of names for possible campaign chairs and suggestions for other key leadership positions based on what he or she has seen and for whom the organization's community showed support with the questionnaires. The consultant will provide copies of this report for you to deliver to the leadership so that you can discuss whether to revise and retest the plans, revise and move forward, or just move forward.

MAIN MESSAGE

After the leadership consolidates the list of wants and needs and collates costs with possible courses of action, allow the organization's community to decide what they will support.

CHAPTER 6
An Overview of the Administrative Issues of the Nonprofit Campaign

At this point, you should have just completed your feasibility study and your campaign consultant has presented you with his or her summary evaluation. Before you go ahead, you will want to meet with your consultant to determine whether you should consider making changes to your plan before moving forward. Because you have done your due diligence and conducted a thorough feasibility study to presell the campaign to your organization and the community, you should not encounter a situation in which the plan has to be changed dramatically. There is a reason why we do things this way. I know of organizations that have approached a feasibility study in a different manner. At the end of the process, they have been forced to abandon their plan or completely rethink their strategy because the study determined that the campaign would not be able to raise nearly enough. I know I must sound like a broken record, but that is yet another reason why we do not ask what someone will give before we know the final plan. There are too many variables that we have yet to consider.

At this point, you will also receive the list of roles and responsibilities for the campaign leaders. Although your consultant should have certain people whom he or she is considering for potential leadership roles in mind, it can be problematic to put those names down in a formal list. You could run into a sticky situation if the list gets out before it is final. Instead, I suggest discussing the potential leaders who have to be recruited first, before anyone else, with the administrator and head of your organization's board. Once you have done that and determined a campaign chair, you can enlist the other individuals on the leadership team. This is where your campaign can truly take off. Identifying and recruiting the best possible individuals is key to conducting a successful campaign. While it may be tempting to ask volunteers to fill leadership roles so that everyone feels involved, I advise you to resist that temptation. Most of the time, the best people for leadership roles are not necessarily those who want the job. Often, the best people to fill these roles are those individuals who feel too busy and overcommitted. However, these may also be the most dedicated people and the kind of people who will do the best job. Nevertheless, as the saying goes, you can lead a horse to water, but you cannot make him drink. Of the many jobs of the campaign consultant is to make the horse thirsty and to get the right people into the right positions.

At this point, we will assume that you have decided to continue with your campaign, either with or without making revisions to your plan. Before you go any further, it is crucial that you fully understand the leadership and administrative positions of the campaign and the responsibilities each person will have.

The point of this chapter is to give you an overview of those responsibilities and provide information about choosing the best leader for each job, the materials you will need, a scale of gifts to achieve the needs you have identified, the campaign calendar, and the responsibility of training and coaching the volunteers on a daily basis.

Now that you have identified and recruited a campaign chairperson, it is time to enlist members of the campaign steering committee. You have identified these people through individual interviews and from the questionnaires you handed out and collected during the focus group meeting, and your consultant has also given you a list of names based on what he or she saw during the feasibility study. Selecting the chairperson first is important because if you select the other members of the committee first, you run the risk of making the campaign chair feel like a figurehead instead of an integral part of the campaign leadership. This lays the groundwork for forming positive personal relationships between the campaign leadership—relationships that are extremely important to a smooth campaign. If the members of the campaign committee feel a personal commitment and dedication to the leadership, they will do everything possible to make sure they do not let the campaign chairperson down.

The campaign plan includes a number of jobs, and you will need to find good, dedicated people to fill all of them. As we saw in the feasibility study, you can engage many members and distribute the workload while creating ownership of the campaign. You may find it challenging to find a place for all those supporters of the organization's community who want to be involved, but this is an opportunity to invite participation from those volunteers who have not found their niche in the organizational community. Some volunteers, for example, may want to help, but traditional volunteer roles either do not fit their schedules or do not play to their strengths. Likewise, instructors or coaches are often overwhelmed with their day to day responsibilities but still feel a desire to give back to the organization in other ways. The campaign could be the perfect opportunity for these members to participate and feel a sense of ownership.

Your consultant should work with you on every step of this process, from choosing the leaders to helping them as they organize each committee. While it is ideal to find an individual person to fill each key position, there are no hard and fast rules that only one person can be named as the chairperson of a particular phase of the campaign. Co-chairs can be a great way to engage more leaders in the campaign, as well as to divide responsibilities and workload. The more people who feel ownership of the campaign, the more successful it will be. Co-chairs also create redundancy at crucial positions so that in the event of illness or travel, there will still be someone filling the position.

In one campaign, we selected and recruited someone who we felt would be an effective pattern gifts chairman. However, due to serious travel demands, he informed us that he did not have enough time to make the campaign a priority for the full time period of the campaign. To ensure that we would benefit from whatever time he could devote to the campaign, we assisted him in finding a co-chair. After a bit more time had passed, it became clear that both co-chairs needed additional help. The head of the organization convinced them to also recruit their wives to help. In the end, the four of them did a great job.

Those people comprising the steering committee should be people of influence who inspire confidence in the success of the capital campaign. You want other members of the organizational community to draw inspiration from the steering committee and to believe that their work will be worthwhile. Past and present leaders of the organization as well as a diverse representation from throughout the community should be represented on the steering committee in order to guide the course of action during the campaign.

Responsibilities:

1. Work closely with the executive director or administrator, Campaign Chairperson(s), and the Campaign Consultant to develop and implement the basic steps of the campaign plan.
2. Help identify and recruit key business and community leaders within the organization's community to serve in leadership positions.
3. Establish a pattern of prompt, thoughtful, and inspirational giving, encouraging others to do the same.
4. Ensure that all committee members have made their pledges.
5. Give the Capital Campaign top priority during the coming weeks and months, performing duties promptly with diligence and enthusiasm. Attendance at all meetings demonstrates hearty backing and support and provides the active guidance necessary for success.
6. Assist in planning the Capital Campaign Kick-off Event.
7. Assure that the entire organizational community is kept informed of the campaign's progress.
8. Help identify and recruit those volunteers who will visit other supporters of the organizaiton and encourage them to participate financially in the campaign.

Specific role responsibilities include:

The executive director or administrator role is one of initiation, inspiration, and support of the capital campaign and the steering committee. The best way to encourage the support of others is to commit to an inspirational gift to the campaign and then announce his or her financial support. Since the executive director's salary is a matter of public record, his or her gift will serve as a benchmark for others. Whether the administrator's salary is $50,000 or $250,000, it is published in the organization's budget and can be accessed by all interested parties. When the campaign begins, it is critical for the administrator to be seen as a leader who is fully committed to the efforts of the campaign. The financial gift of the administrator can be inspirational to others. It can serve as the first step in a successful campaign.

In a recent campaign in a small nonprofit where the administrator made $50,000 a year, he asked me what other administrators had given to campaigns. I told him that the amount varied based on the ability of the administrator to give. He asked me what I thought he would need to contribute over the five years to set a good example of inspirational giving. I told him that a $25,000 gift from him during that time would be inspirational and would encourage others to give selflessly as well. He took a deep breath and told me that he would discuss it with his wife. The next day, when he and his wife were asked for their pledge, he informed us that he was deeply committed to the campaign and instead of the discussed $25,000, they pledged $30,000 over five years. The community was inspired and they ultimately raised significant funds, far surpassing their goal.

The executive director or administrator must also attend all of the steering committee meetings as a visual example of support for the campaign. If people see the administrator attending every meeting and being involved at every level, they will believe in the goals and mission of the campaign. The administrator will be crucial in helping recruit others to lead the campaign. Through personal interactions with other members of the organization's community, he or she will create a sense of understanding and support for the campaign. By using personal stories and connections to other people who care about the organization, the administrator will participate in solicitation visits as needed and work closely with the campaign consultant to assist in decision-making. He or she will also be apprised of various campaign issues, typically in daily meetings with the campaign consultant.

As part of a rural campaign, the administrator and I would meet every morning. In addition, we would meet just before the Thursday night campaign meetings to discuss any last-minute concerns. After the meeting ended and the group dispersed, the administrator and I met up at a coffee shop to talk about the meeting and discuss strategy for the upcoming week. While it may seem like an excessive number of meetings, they provided a great opportunity to keep the administrator on track in all aspects of the campaign. He never felt out of the loop and was able to speak knowledgably with anyone who asked about the campaign. The campaign was a great success, and the organization ultimately enjoyed a highly successful campaign. Fourteen years later, the administrator and I are still in contact, and we often discuss the successful campaign and our experiences together.

The Campaign Chairperson is the volunteer leader for the effort who does not work directly for the organization. He or she must be an individual whom the organization's board and administration see as a natural leader within the community. This could be a volunteer or supporter with special ties to and interest in the organization. It is best if the person has shown an interest in the campaign, but there are times when the person you choose may need to be coaxed into assuming this leadership position. However, it is important to listen to your volunteers. If the chair-select informs you that he or she has neither the time nor the inclination to work on the project, try to find another leader. You do not want to force this responsibility on someone who does not feel able to commit to it. This job requires a serious commitment, and like the executive director, the campaign chair should be prepared to give an inspirational gift to the campaign. He or she should preside over all steering committee meetings and help identify, recruit, and motivate other leaders to participate in the campaign. This is why a successful constituency could be an excellent choice for this position. He or she can be inspirational to other members of the organization—a visual representation of the success and potential of the organization. The consultant will work as the campaign chair's right arm, making sure that the chair has all of the support that he or she needs.

In a large nonprofit campaign, the administrator decided who he wanted to serve as the campaign chair even before the feasibility study was completed. His nominee was a well-known and well-respected business leader in the community who had been involved in the organization years before. The administrator and business leader held a series of private meetings and the administrator learned that the man would accept the position reluctantly but was not willing to make a large gift or participate in all committee meetings. The business leader was notable, and the administrator felt that having the man's name associated with the campaign would be enough. As we neared the conclusion of the focus group meetings, the administrator informed me of his choice. I had recently completed reviewing the questionnaires that had been filled out during the focus group meetings, and I had only seen the man's name mentioned twice. I was concerned, knowing this situation was a recipe for disaster. Thinking quickly, I offered the administrator an alternate, a committed, well-respected member of the community whose name had been raised in numerous focus group meetings as a respected leader. This person had also expressed a keen interest in leading the campaign during my personal interview with them. However, against my advice, the administrator refused. My arguments for the person I suggested as opposed to the high-profile administrator's choice were ignored. Finally, at my urging, the administrator agreed to allow the other member to serve as co-chair along with his choice. As the campaign progressed, the reluctant business leader performed exactly as I had anticipated and was not a force for the campaign. Instead, the co-chair carried the campaign and led a highly successful effort, something in which the reluctant chair took great pride.

The **Advance Gifts Chairperson** is responsible for securing major gifts that will represent 50 to 60 percent of the campaign goal. Like all campaign leaders, the advance gifts chairperson should be willing to make a gift of his or her own. The chair is responsible for recruiting people of influence and affluence who will feel comfortable asking peers to make inspirational gifts to ensure the success of the campaign. He or she will divide the selected members into teams, each with a captain and team members to call on the identified business and community leaders. The team captain will solicit pledges from the team members. He or she should make sure that adequate orientation, training, and coaching are provided to team members before they select which prospects they will target for donations. The advance gifts chairperson should also oversee the selection of prospects to make sure that team members are matched with prospects in the most beneficial way possible. This campaign phase happens before the kick-off event, so it is important that this chairperson be ready to hit the ground running when the organization's board decides to go forward with the plan of campaign. The advance gifts chairperson works very closely with the campaign consultant and is responsible for announcing the goal of the campaign in advance of the Kick-off Event.

One board member wanted desperately to be part of the campaign leadership. However, he was concerned that he would not be the most helpful, since he could only afford to give $25,000 to the campaign. While I thought this was a generous gift indeed, it was not enough to reach the level necessary for the advance gifts chairperson. Nevertheless, he desperately wanted the position, and he told me that if I helped him get it, he would write a check the next day for the full amount. This did not sound right to me because, as an experienced fundraiser, I knew that anyone who could write a check for $25,000 at one time could give significantly more than that over five years. I told him this and challenged him to extend his gift over five years and contribute $100,000 in total. He hemmed and hawed and told me about other people he knew who could more easily afford that amount. I told him that if he were to ask another potential donor for $100,000, he would need to pledge that amount himself to lend legitimacy to the campaign. I also reminded him that he was under no obligation to take the position, but if he did not, I needed to find someone to give at that level who could challenge others to do the same. Before we ended our meeting, he agreed to the $100,000 pledge. Once he had done that, he was able to call on others to match his generosity. Ultimately, he became a great advocate for the campaign and was heard to say repeatedly, "If not us, who? And if not now, when?" Sometimes, people need to be encouraged or gently pushed to do all they can for the campaign. While I would never advocate asking people for more than they can afford to give, this man's offer to write a check for the entire amount told me that he could certainly afford it. In the end, he made a very generous gift and served as an excellent Advance Gifts Chairperson for this very successful campaign.

The **Pattern Gift Chairperson's** role is to enlist other top leaders who are capable of soliciting gifts from prospects who may be able to contribute in an intermediate financial range. Pattern gifts will represent 30 to 35 percent of the total campaign goal. Of course, the pattern gifts chairperson must make an inspirational gift of his or her own. Like the advance gifts chair, he or she will identify teams and team captains to ensure that no team member has to solicit more than five to ten prospects. You do not want to overload people with prospects. Asking for pledges is taxing and takes an emotional investment both from the person soliciting the donation and the person giving it. Make sure that no team member is overburdened. The pattern gifts chairperson makes sure that the consultant provides all team members with adequate orientation, training, and coaching prior to selecting prospects. In conjunction with the consultant, the pattern gifts chairperson oversees the selection of prospects to help ensure that the right team members are matched up to the right prospects. The team captain will solicit pledges from the team members.

The **Mission or Vision Chairperson's** responsibilities include recruiting a small group of members who can assist with the various responsibilities of this committee. These responsibilities include preparing a mission statement that can be used throughout the campaign, such as during campaign update meetings, community meetings, and board meetings. He or she collects fifteen to twenty written testimonials from various organization members that will be used to validate their endorsement of the project, their personal development decisions, and the importance of the nonprofit in their lives and the community. This chairperson should plan to address campaign leaders immediately prior to the victory team visitation phase. This should last no longer than three minutes for each steering committee meeting and the campaign training meetings. He or she works with the administrator to recruit and solicit speakers for meetings throughout the campaign. This is an important position to keep the focus of the campaign on organizational issues.

A small nonprofit was having a difficult time recruiting someone to serve as the mission committee chair. A male board member had recently dealt with a difficult business situation and relied on volunteering for the organization's theater component to help him through it. The administrator, a very insightful man, had seen the man's great dedication through his reliance on and involvement with the organization. The man had lost his footing in the community, and the administrator saw his involvement in the campaign as an opportunity for him to right the ship and regain his standing. He invited this man to serve as the mission committee chair. The man was deeply moved, as he felt the organization was extremely important in his life and embraced the job, wanting to give back.

Ideally, the **Publicity Chairperson** should bbe someone who is familiar with public relations. His or her responsibilities include working with the campaign chairperson(s) and the consultant to prepare all of the campaign materials—including fact sheets—as well as articles that can appear in the nonprofit's newsletter and bulletin. This person coordinates all public announcements about the plans and progress reports concerning the campaign and prepares news releases and disseminates them to the appropriate media outlets as needed. The publicity chairperson also visits organizational planning groups and volunteer and community events to communicate the aims, purposes, and goals of the campaign. He or she also creates the capital campaign goal chart.

The **Kick-off Event Chairperson(s)** is responsible for the Kick-off Event, which will be discussed in detail in Chapter 9. The chairperson(s) will work closely with the campaign chairperson(s) and the consultant to coordinate the event. This chairperson is responsible for recruiting a small committee to address invitations (volunteers can be useful in this capacity), selecting the menu for the event, providing decorations,

76

securing a speaker system and other visual aid equipment, and planning for nursery/childcare. This chairperson also arranges transportation for the elderly and handicapped, forms a telephone committee to call each family, encourages attendance, recruits members of the steering committee and other members of the nonprofit community to serve as hosts/hostesses, and coordinates with the steering committee regarding the dinner program. Obviously, someone who is familiar with event planning would be excellent in this position, but as long as the kick-off event chairperson works closely with the campaign consultant, he or she can plan a successful event.

The **Treasurer/Auditor** certifies the consultant's record of pledges, deposits money as it is received, and keeps an accurate record of the total funds received and disbursed. As a result, someone with a financial background is especially useful in this position. The treasurer/auditor is also responsible for coordinating the transfer of stocks, bonds, and other marketable assets, making disbursements, and maintaining a record of campaign expenses. It is also his or her responsibility to audit records and pledge cards at the end of the campaign and to prepare a proper summary, required by the consultant and the steering committee. Proper records of financial transactions are crucial to ensuring proper accounting of the campaign, so making sure that you have appointed a responsible, experienced treasurer/auditor is critical. This person will also work closely with the finance committee.

Finance Committee: Depending on the size of the organization, a Finance Committee may already exist. If one does not, an ad hoc committee might be established for the duration of the campaign, or the treasurer may serve as the Finance Committee. At all phases of the campaign, the committee must accomplish the following things:

- Approve the budget
- Pay all bills
- Monitor and audit all gifts made, including in-kind contributions, cash, and pledges;
- Provide an account, in writing, of the status and total of all pledges and amounts paid prior to the conclusion of the campaign.

Memorials Committee: With the help of the campaign consultant and the campaign chairs, the memorials committee will identify naming opportunities and the gift level associated with each of these opportunities. This committee will also identify a method for recognizing memorial gifts to ensure that each gift is recognized in the way the donor intended.

This committee is responsible for establishing a memorials book with appropriate and complete entries honoring all memorial gifts, writing thank-you letters for each gift, and, in collaboration with the publicity committee, developing memorial gifts recognition. Your consultant can help you to determine what naming opportunities might be available and what level gift would be appropriate for these opportunities. For instance, if you are building a new auditorium or other building facilities, these are a common opportunity for naming. Additionally, large memorial gifts can be honored with entire building dedications. Slightly smaller donations can be acknowledged with room names—for instance, the new job training center can be named after a memorial donation of someone who supported workplace advancement. Regardless of whether your organization will accept naming opportunities or establish a memorial committee as part of the campaign, it is always appropriate to encourage that gifts be made in honor of someone.

The Materials of the Campaign

As with all things pertaining to the campaign, the materials must reflect the personality of your organization and the community in which you operate. The view book, the pledge card, the visitor's handbook, the campaign brochure, and the kick-off event program will be discussed in detail. It is imperative to begin the design process of each of these as soon as the decision to move forward is made. Campaigns are short, and both design and printing take time—often more time than you think.

The View Book: The View Book is one of the best ways to send a clear and consistent message regarding the campaign. It presents the case for support in presentation format and can be used as a script by volunteers when they make their visits to solicit donations. The view book is used during the advance gift phase of the campaign. The consultant should have experience creating view books and will lay out, in detail, everything that goes into it, including sample letters from the organization's administration and campaign chair. However, it is important that the personality of the nonprofit be reflected in the view book. This is not a simple cut and paste template. It should feel as though it truly represents your organization. All of the pages should be bound and easy to flip through. Many of the creative design people with whom I have consulted encourage the inclusion of a pocket in the back for all the included materials. To me, this makes sense and makes organization easier. The view book should also be personalized for the person being called on. This is more expensive, of course, than a simple printing run, so personalized view books should be reserved for the most affluent and influential members of the organization's community, which usually amounts to about 10 percent of the community.

Recently, I was told about an inexperienced consultant who did not use a view book at all. Instead, he went on his campaign visits with a handful of organizational newsletters, assuming that they told the story of the nonprofit sufficiently. The campaign was not successful; existing newsletters are not inspirational.

The view book and ultimately the brochure, should be designed with the understanding that it will be a clear and concise case for support. For the view book to be used as a useful script for the volunteers making the visits, the following order of pages makes the most sense:

- Mission statement
- Inspirational letter from the president of the organization's board or head administrator
- Hearty endorsement from Campaign Chair and board chair
- History of the organization
- Proposed new floor plans
- Site plan of the property
- Elevated rendering of the proposed new facilities
- Estimate of costs
- Memorial and naming opportunities, if appropriate
- Capital Campaign vs. annual campaign differences (see below)
- Explanation that gifts can be made over a three- to five-year period
- Listing of all organization and campaign leaders

An excerpt from a View Book explains the difference between capital giving and annual pledging. Capital giving differs from annual pledging in several ways.

Capital giving:

- Takes place only when absolutely necessary
- Spreads out payments during a much longer period
- Is in response to an urgent need
- Seeks larger amounts than annual budgets can cover

- Requires a planned, sacrificial, and inspirational effort, and often involves giving of real estate, securities, life insurance, or other tangible assets
- Is over and above annual giving. Therefore, customary giving habits will not produce the desired results and assure a victory for your organization's building campaign.

Some larger nonprofits with advanced audiovisual departments are now designing videos to spread the message of their campaign. If done properly, this can be an extremely effective tool; however, you must ensure that your video production is high quality and be certain that your organization's message comes through. It is tempting to give in to new technology and flash, but do not forget the substance.

I recently watched a video for a nonprofit in Florida, and it was so beautifully done that it brought a tear to my eye. The downside is that videos take a lot of time and money to do right. Videos do not replace personal visits, nor should the visit consist solely of watching the video together and then handing the person called on a pledge card. Some consulting firms push the development of a video, but I do not personally believe that a video is going to make someone pledge who wouldn't otherwise do so.

However, in the case of large nonprofits, videos can be useful to help spread the word and create excitement for the project. Additionally, people can refer back to the video—the shared experience—when discussing the campaign. Finally, if your organization is engaged with outside counsel for your campaign, make certain that the firm encouraging the video production does not own the production company or have an agreement to be compensated for every organization it convinces to make a video. This is a clear conflict of interest and a sign that your consultant does not have your organization's best interests at heart.

The Pledge Card

An effective campaign program will create pledge cards personalized with the name and address of the family to be visited. We do this so that we avoid duplicate campaign visits. There is nothing less professional than being visited twice for the same pledge because the campaign does not have clear records. Personalized pledge cards are the way we avoid duplicate campaign visits. The campaign should use the organization's entire mailing list for the development of prospects. Many nonprofits make the mistake of planning to ask only involved families or families who are currently utilizing the organization to support the campaign. However, I have found that it is not only financially prudent to include all of the nonprofit community members and past leaders, but it is also the moral and inclusive thing to do. Long time supporters often have great pride in their organization; they will be hurt if they are left out.

The pledge card should be printed on card stock with the organization's logo and the theme of the campaign. The name of the family or person being visited should either be printed on the card with a computer or attached with a sticker. Avoid hand-writing the names on the cards. It may seem as though it gives the cards a personal touch, but in reality, it looks unprofessional.

The card should be able to fit in your pocket or purse—as that is where it will stay during the presentation—and should have a perforated tear-off stub with the suggested level of giving. The stub is removed before the visit. The tear-off serves as a reminder to the visitor of the suggested level of giving.

The card should include a description of the amount the donor is pledging and of how the donor intends to pay the pledge: by monthly or annual installments or in a lump sum. Some nonprofits allow pledges by credit or debit card payments, but there is usually a fee associated with those payments. The card should have a place for a signature. In recent campaigns, we have also been adding space on the back of the pledge card for the donor to note if the gift is in memory or honor of someone.

A few years ago, one organization insisted that the pledge card be oversized to stress the importance of the gifts to the campaign. They believed that a large pledge card would send the subliminal message that a large donation was appreciated. Instead, most of these oversized pledge cards ended up torn or tattered because they were oversized and did not easily fit into pockets or purses. In my experience, the size of the pledge card does not influence the size of the gift; the reminder is good but a visual cue is not necessary.

The Visitor's Handbook

The Visitor's Handbook is a reference and practice guide that includes information about the consultant and the leaders of the campaign as well as frequently asked questions with proposed answers. This book should be reviewed in depth before making a campaign visit. Ensure that your campaign volunteers review the material in this book so that they can best answer any questions that might arise. There will, of course, be unexpected questions at times, but prepared is always better. This book should be semiformal or bound so that it does not come apart. It should not be stapled loose-leaf papers. Many people will have their hands on it; you will want it to be sturdy.

The Campaign Brochure

The campaign brochure contains all of the same essential elements as the view book. However, it is not personalized, so it can be mass-produced. All members of the community who are not given a view book will receive a campaign brochure. You can choose whether or not this brochure is distributed at the kick-off dinner. Just as with the other aspects of the campaign, it needs to fit the personality of your organization and the community. Your consultant should lay out the format and text of the brochure to be approved by the campaign steering committee. While it is important for the brochure to be attractive, it should also be practical. That is, do not create a large, unwieldy brochure full of glossy photographs with little information. The brochure, like the view book, will be used as a script for the visitors. You will want to make it as easy as possible for them to do so. The brochure should present the information in a clear and concise manner.

To maximize usefulness, the pages of the campaign brochure should be in the following order:

- Mission statement
- Letter from the organization's board chair or head administrator
- Hearty endorsement from Campaign Chair and Board Chair

- History of the nonprofit
- Floor plans
- Site plan
- Elevated rendering
- Estimate of costs
- Memorial and naming opportunities
- Capital Campaign vs. annual campaign differences
- Explanation that gifts can be made over a three-to five-year period
- Listing of all of the organization and campaign leaders

For a nonprofit campaign in Florida, the publicity committee went against our strong advice and created a brochure that was extremely elegant and quite beautiful. However, it contained no essential information regarding the campaign. In the back was a small pocket filled with the renderings of the proposed building and the cost estimates. Every time people opened the brochure, a page or two from the back would fall out and was often lost. Although the organization was complimented on the appearance of the brochure, it became a sore spot for the campaign because of the high cost and low functionality of the large brochures. The return on investment was not good, and the brochures were not nearly as useful as they should have been.

The Kick-off Event Program

I have found that a simple way to set up the program for the kick-off event is to use a folded 8½×11–inch card stock page—with a picture representative of the organization on the cover, the mission statement of the nonprofit on the inside left, the program on the inside right, and perhaps a note of thanks from the campaign chairs on the back cover. To keep costs low, you should use only one additional color. It is not necessary for this program to be extravagant or ornate. You want only to present the information.

At a campaign Kick-off Event in Virginia, instead of card stock, a bookmark-size piece of flimsy paper was distributed to people as they arrived at the event. This paper was intended to serve as the event program. However, nowhere on the slip of paper did the name of the organization appear. Instead, the paper contained information regarding the entertainment. This was not ideal.

The Scale of Gifts

A good consulting firm will provide you with a scale of gifts necessary to achieve your needs. The scale is a listing of dollar amounts in pledges that are required to reach a particular dollar goal. Your consultant will help you to understand why this particular scale is appropriate, given the size and scope of your campaign. In all of our campaigns, we strive to get a lead gift of 10 to 20 percent, as it sets a good example for gifts that follow; we have nearly always been successful. After the lead gift, there should be two gifts that each represent 5 percent of the goal. The next two to three gifts should represent 2 to 3 percent of the goal, and so on.

During a client project with fewer than three thousand members in the community, the campaign leaders determined through their focus group meetings that they needed to raise $25 million. The campaign committee asked me to prepare a scale of gifts to see if they would be justified in setting $25 million as their goal. I did as they asked and told them that in order to do so, the school would need a lead gift of $5 million and three $1 million gifts. The leaders balked at the amounts and said that there was no way the community could support that level of giving. I told them that that was fine; if they could not support those gifts, they could adjust the plan to better reflect what the community was capable of doing. However, I recommended that before they decided what the community could not do, they allow the community the chance to disappoint them. The leaders went forward with the requests as detailed and every gift amount was met. At the kick-off event, over $12 million of their $25 million goal had been pledged.

Typically, if you are seeking to raise $5 million, a lead gift of between $500,000 and $1 million is required, followed by two $250,000 pledges and ten $100,000 pledges. Remember that these amounts are being pledged over a three- to five-year period, so it is not as if you are expecting a donor to write you a check for $1 million all at once.

Once you have determined your scale of gifts, you must begin the sometimes-contentious process of identifying who in the nonprofit community should be called upon for the larger gifts. When working with various campaigns, I have found that there are two typical responses: nonprofits that say there are a number of community members who could make large pledges and organizations that claim that no one in the community can. I remind nonprofits that these requests are based on a scale of gifts to meet their particular needs. These numbers do not appear out of thin air; they are based on the concrete needs of your organizational community as determined by your focus group meetings. If your community does not have people who can make these gifts, then we should readjust the expectations and make some decisions about which are the most urgent priorities.

Scale of Gifts NEEDED TO RAISE $6 MILLION

ADVANCE GIFTS PHASE

Amount	No. of Gifts	No. of Prospects	To Raise $	Total $
$700,000	1	5	700,000	700,000
300,000	2	4	600,000	1,300,000
200,000	3	5	600,000	1,900,000
150,000	4	10	600,000	2,500,000
100,000	5	10	500,000	3,000,000

PHASE TOTAL $3,000,000

PATTERN GIFT PHASE

Amount	No. of Gifts	No. of Prospects	To Raise $	Total $
$75,000	10	20	750,000	750,000
50,000	15	30	750,000	1,500,000
35,000	20	40	700,000	2,200,000

PHASE TOTAL $2,200,000

VICTORY TEAMS PHASE

Amount	No. of Gifts	No. of Prospects	To Raise $	Total $
$25,000	20	40	500,000	500,000
10,000	20	40	200,000	700,000
5,000	20	40	100,000	800,000

PHASE TOTAL $800,000

GRAND TOTAL $6,000,000

The Appraisals Process

Before you begin asking members of the community to donate to your organization's campaign, you should conduct a complete review process to help determine what potential donors might consider contributing if they were committed to supporting the campaign to the best of their ability. This process can be difficult, as no one is familiar with someone else's true ability to contribute to a campaign. We should encourage inspirational and sacrificial giving during a capital campaign. Therefore, people need to know what range of gift to "consider" to best help the nonprofit organization reach its goal. Only by presenting the request for gifts at specific levels can you succeed, because only by presenting target figures will you receive more than token contributions. If you leave the amount open and do not suggest an amount, many people will fail to grasp the importance of the commitment and will make only a small, token donation.

It is, however, important to remember that the "asking amount" is neither an assessment nor a requirement; it is a level of gift to consider that will help donors make an educated decision regarding their gift. By no means should your campaign require anyone to make a donation of any amount. There are always mitigating circumstances of which we cannot always be aware. As visitors learn in our coaching sessions, "consider" is the key word in properly asking for pledges.

Every prospective donor or member of the organization's community must be reviewed on an individual basis. Appraise prospects based on the level of gift they "could" give if they were 100 percent behind the project. Use the best knowledge and information you have at your disposal to review potential donors and make educated asks.

Be fair. Remember to apply the golden rule: review or appraise each person on your donor list as you would like to be appraised. Targets should be a stretch, but should not be out of reach. If too many people make pledges over or at their asking amount, we have not challenged them to stretch in their giving and should reconsider our evaluation process.

It is only natural that many people's first response to this approach is discomfort. Very few people are comfortable with the concept of targeting donors, but in truth, if there is to be any chance of reaching your campaign goal, presenting targets must be done. No campaign, whether for a hospital, church, or school, can reasonably expect to succeed without presenting to potential donors the targets that have been established in relation to the total needs.

When we are discussing an individual organization's campaign, we must first acknowledge that the potential donors are both financially capable and generous. However, a campaign effort still presents us with the challenge of having to raise the total funds necessary over three years, with some asking to extend the payment period to five years. During a capital campaign, where asking amounts are presented, it helps to keep these principles in mind:

- It is important to stress equal levels of sacrifice, not equal giving. Each donor has a different set of circumstances. Asking donors to consider gifts of various amounts reflects our sensitivity to this issue. Per capita giving is not productive for fundraising, nor is it right to ask all donors, regardless of their circumstances, to consider giving the same amount. It also appears impersonal and as though people are not being considered as individuals.

- Usually, our giving to any charitable or nonprofit institution is based on what we want to give. The "asking amounts" established by developing a thoughtful and reasonable scale of gifts for your capital campaign and presented to the organization's community by campaign visitors reflect what the nonprofit needs to fund the project.

- This "asking amount" is a figure that we are asking donors to consider. It is not what you are supposed to give. It is not what you are expected to give. It is simply a target for you to consider. There should be no pressure to meet or exceed the asked amount.

- Because we usually need inspirational and sacrificial giving to reach our goal, some asking amounts will be more than some donors can give. The main point is to stretch in your giving toward the target amount as much as possible.

The campaigns my firm conducts never determine asking amounts by zip code, street name, or tax records. Solely considering someone's financial balance sheet is not a sufficient way to determine an appropriate asking amount. Instead, the amounts should be arrived at by a small group of individuals who know the organization's community or constituency intimately, who can intelligently and knowledgably consider the scale and determine which donors should be asked to consider various levels of gifts. Finally, keeping all discussions and considerations absolutely confidential is crucial. This process will only be successful if everyone involved is shown the respect he or she deserves.

In a campaign at a small nonprofit in Florida, the treasurer asked if it would be appropriate to do a financial review of everyone based on information purchased from an investigative organization. I immediately stopped that line of discussion. It can be incredibly damaging to a campaign and your continued relationship to your organizational community if members perceive that you have done background checks on them. No one wants to feel investigated. Contributing to the campaign is voluntary and should be kept that way.

Campaign Calendar

Once you have made the decision to move forward, your consultant should set up a campaign calendar. At a glance, the consultant should be able to tell you how many weeks you will need to meet personally with all of your potential donors, because that is the true goal of the campaign, not the amount. Frequently, I encounter nonprofits that want to wait for the "perfect" time to conduct their campaign. However, the time of year is not important, even if you are working against a seasonal calendar and various vacations. If you try to meet some artificial deadline to be inclusive of some members, you will lose the interest of other members. Weather may determine the timing of your campaign, especially if you are in the north. It could be difficult for volunteers to make face-to-face visits in January in that setting. Nevertheless, if you intend to meet with every prospective donor individually, individual schedules can be accommodated. Do not worry too much about vacations and holidays in the campaign calendar; they can be worked around. In most cases, the campaign calendar will be determined by the urgency of the project.

Duration of the campaign. Like the length of the Feasibility Study, the length of the Capital Campaign will vary based on the size of the organization's community and the financial objective of the campaign. You want to allow enough time to ensure that every prospective donor can be personally visited, but you do not want to burn out your volunteers by extending the effort unnecessarily. The average campaign may be twenty to thirty weeks. Anyone who is involved in the campaign, especially the campaign steering committee, will be expected to make the campaign effort a top priority. However, if the campaign is going to last over a year or two, it is unreasonable to expect these individuals to make the effort their top priority. Before the campaign even begins, the length of time of the campaign and what is expected of everyone involved must be made very clear. If conducted properly, the length of the campaign should be determined by the amount of money that is needed to be raised. The method in which people are asked and the length of time needed to ensure all prospective individuals are visited also drive the length of the campaign. However, a longer campaign may only result in your organization needing to pay for a consultant for a longer period of time.

During a campaign in California, the chairman decided to reduce the number of visiting weeks from twenty to fifteen on his own. I knew that the organization could never finish the necessary visits in fifteen weeks. I further knew that after our consultant left, no more visits would be conducted and the organization would not reach its goal. I wanted the nonprofit to succeed, but I also wanted a success for our firm. Because the chairman would not listen to me, I sent a letter to the steering committee congratulating the members on their kick-off event and reminding them that to reach their goal, they would need to schedule the full twenty weeks. At the next campaign committee meeting, the members unanimously decided that the campaign effort would last twenty weeks and requested that our consultant remain with them for the full time period. Though overruling the chairman made the campaign a bit difficult, volunteers were pleased we remained on site to help make personal visits, and ultimately, they were able to visit all prospective donors of the organization's community and reached their goal.

Part of staying on track with the campaign calendar is ensuring that your volunteers know that they are the linchpins in your effort. Your volunteers must feel appreciated and valued. Without their commitment to calling on the nonprofit community, the task would be overwhelming for the campaign leadership. Volunteers are difficult to manage, because you are not paying them to do a job; they are participating out of their commitment to the organization. However, if volunteers are not making their calls in a timely manner or if they are not asking in the right way, you must stop them and either retrain them or simply thank them for their effort and recruit new volunteers. It is difficult to "fire" someone whom you are not paying, but there are ways to tactfully deal with the situation. It is worse to have someone calling on people improperly than to have a delay in the calendar. When recruiting your volunteers, they should know that this is a real commitment, and they should be fully devoted to the campaign.

MAIN MESSAGE

Those involved in the campaign are making a commitment that cannot be taken lightly. There is much to do; either you will do it all or you will recruit the right people to help. With a good consultant, identifying those people will be easier and will ultimately ensure the success of the campaign. The materials used in the campaign are nearly as important as the individual who personally delivers the message. Take the time and care to create the best materials possible to ensure a smooth and successful campaign.

CHAPTER 7
The Right Way:
How to Ask for Financial Support

A board member had heard that a friend in the community had recently made a $500,000 commitment to a new project with another organization in town. Surprised, the board member approached the friend to ask if it was true. The individual had never given significantly to any of their programs in the past. The man confirmed that it was, in fact, true. When the board member asked why he would give so much money to another project in the community, the man replied, "Because they asked me."

After conducting your feasibility study and receiving the final report from your consultant, you have determined that your nonprofit community supports the ideas and spirit of your proposed campaign. Now you have to ask the organization's board members to consider making a pledge to the campaign. You asked them personally to be part of the feasibility study. It is now time to personally ask them to be part of the capital campaign by making a multiyear pledge. While it may seem uncomfortable, you must give all board members and all prospective donors an opportunity to be part of the campaign. You may feel that after they have spent so much of their time consulting on the campaign and working to create a plan, the last thing you want to do is ask them for money, but in reality, capital giving is part of being involved.

Approaching your constituency for pledges shows that you value not only their input but also their contributions and that you want them to be a critical part of the success of the campaign.

My wife and I moved into a new church community, and to our great surprise, in our second week, the pastor announced that they were in the midst of a $6 million capital campaign. I called the pastor to let him know that I had some experience in fundraising. He thanked me for the call and told me that the church had already engaged with outside counsel. I offered to assist in the campaign and gave him my contact information, which he assured me that he would pass along to the lay leadership. My wife, Molly, and I picked up a campaign brochure to familiarize ourselves with the objectives of the campaign and began to consider what we could contribute to the campaign, although we were not certain of the pledging period. Over the coming days and weeks, we continued to discuss what we could contribute, and each time the amount was slightly increased. To our surprise, no one ever called to ask us to help make calls or to ask us for a pledge. We were shocked one Sunday at a church service when the pastor announced the end of the successful campaign. He announced that they had reached the goal of $3 million. He invited everyone who had not yet contributed to fill out pledge cards in the pews. Needless to say, we were very disappointed and did not feel that our contribution was either necessary or wanted. It is a lesson I pass along to every client. Our gift may not have been among the largest, but it would have been meaningful to us if we had been personally visited and asked for a pledge.

The point of this chapter is to teach you some of the key principles of asking for a gift. Some consultants might advise you to simply leave a pledge card, while others will encourage you to write a heart-wrenching letter, appealing to someone's emotional side. While both letters and pledge cards have their place, I will tell you that no letter has ever been more effective than someone whose life has been touched by the organization calling someone else to request a thoughtful donation to the organization that has meant so much to them. This is the area of my approach with which nonprofits tend to be the most uncomfortable. The idea of asking each donor in the community for a gift can make them cringe. They are often uncomfortable with both the work involved in making the visit and with the idea of asking someone for a specific and large amount of money. To help them better understand it, I often explain it this way in campaign sales presentations: "How many of you in the room would be offended if someone you know from the organization called and asked if he could come by to discuss the campaign?" No one has ever raised his/her hand. I point out that nearly everyone else will feel the same way. The important thing to remember is that the right person is chosen to ask the prospective campaign donor. It should be someone who has already made a pledge, can articulate the plans of the campaign, and knows the donor being called upon. Personal connections are important and go a long way toward soliciting successful pledges. Just as your volunteers and campaign committee want to feel as though their input and experience is valued, so do the individuals in your community. Making them feel as though their contribution is valued is an extremely important part of a successful campaign.

On one campaign I worked on, I explained to the committee the proper way to make a campaign call. However, shortly thereafter, a campaign chair decided to deviate from the path. He was scheduled to call on a very prominent member of the community, and he wanted to make the call himself because he wanted to be the one who brought in the lead gift; he was certain this man would donate a large gift. At the committee meeting after his visit, we all waited to hear how his meeting went. When the chair arrived, he explained that instead of visiting the man, he had sent him a letter and the view book. My heart sank; I knew no good would come from this. I remained silent as the chair explained that he was certain he would get a very positive response, despite the impersonal nature of the contact. Before the meeting ended, I was forced to remind the committee that this was not the way to make the calls. I predicted that the letter would not solicit a pledge. The chair was angry with me for pointing out the flaws in his plan. However, the following week, he got a response to his letter. It was a terse reply stating that the man had received it, would consider it, and was very surprised that a gift of this size would be addressed in a written request. Ultimately, the man made no pledge, proving once again that a personal touch means everything.

Administratively, there are only two essential elements to being a good volunteer:

1. Report on every pledge card you agreed to take. If you do not visit your prospects in person, no one else will.

For one campaign on which I consulted, the chair decided that he wanted to personally call on the six largest prospects. Two weeks into the campaign, he had not made any of his calls and few others had made theirs. I called the organization's administrator and requested an emergency meeting. When everyone was gathered together, I told them that I was not interested in wasting their money and that if they were not going to make their calls, there was no point in my staying around. Faced with losing a consultant, they all agreed to make their calls in the next week. As the week passed, I called the campaign chair and learned that he had yet to make any of his calls. He made excuses and again promised to make the calls. I called him back and told him that I would happily take back the pledge cards and materials he had selected. He was surprised, yet grateful and I was determined to get these six affluent members called on in order to give the campaign a jump start. I redistributed his pledge cards and materials to two other members, who made the calls in the next few days. They both secured large gifts, and ultimately, the campaign was a terrific success.

2. Work only from the pledge cards prepared by the office. This way we avoid duplication. If you want to call on a particular person, you should check with the office to make sure another visitor has not selected the prospect. Nothing undermines the personal touch of an in-person visit more than duplicate visits and being inconsiderate of someone's time.

In a nonprofit campaign, a member of the board who was a stockbroker chose the pledge card of a wealthy community family. However, he had ulterior motives for wanting to meet this influential family. This was clear from the beginning, and when the board member made his visit, it got off track quickly and the representative from the wealthy family ended up declining to sign his pledge card. The stockbroker returned from the visit, announcing that the wealthy family had no interest in the campaign. A short while later, the wealthy man's wife complained to the board president that during the visit, the stockbroker was trying to get her husband's business and had not seemed focused on the campaign; that is why they had not made a pledge. To follow up, another member of the campaign committee made a call. In contrast to the stockbroker's visit, she was welcomed into the family's home and enjoyed a lovely evening. The couple ended up pledging $100,000 to the campaign.

In order to make certain that a call is successful, use these **Ten Guiding Principles** for everyone in the campaign. Everyone from the nonprofit board president to a volunteer on any of the committees should follow these guidelines.

The Ten Guiding Principles

1. *Make your own gift first.* Carefully consider your own inspirational gift before you visit with others. Then you can say, "Won't you join me?" You cannot expect others to donate to something that you yourself have not supported.

2. *Use a team approach.* Experience shows that teams get better attention, more serious consideration, and better results than individuals do working on their own. Make sure that your fellow visitor has also made a campaign pledge and be certain to practice the presentation together so that it is coordinated and not redundant.

3. *Be informed.* Understand the campaign objective and be able to articulate it before you go out on a call. Practice your presentation so that you are not caught off guard. The View Book or brochure will give you the necessary information. Study them thoroughly so that you are knowledgeable about the campaign.

4. *Be proud of your task and be yourself.* You are providing friends with an opportunity to share with you and others in the future of the organization. This is not a donation; it is an investment in the future of the nonprofit and an improvement to the community. Tell the story in your own style. Your conviction and enthusiasm will be the most important ingredients in your presentation. If the people were not able to attend the Kick-off Event, share some of the stories from the event with them.

5. *Be committed.* You do not need to be a professional salesperson to be a successful campaign visitor. Remember that you will be visiting friends who are interested in the future of the organization. They have many of the same concerns as you do. Do not give in to the temptation of procrastination. It will only add to your anxiety of going on the first call and can slow down your momentum. One good pledge, along with your own, will set the standard for others and boost your morale. Remember, every prospective donor

is important, and every gift is necessary for success. *Never* try to solicit by telephone or by letter. Go in person and be excited about the visit.

6. ***Ask for a specific gift.*** Seek a decision of the proper level. Begin at the high end of the range. It is next to impossible to begin at the lowest level and move up. If you attempt to do so, you will likely only receive token gifts. Even if the gift is much less than the request, donors should feel good about what they can do, not sorry about what they cannot do. Never make anyone feel bad for the amount of their gift. Remind them that every gift is valued.

7. ***Be informed of various donation methods!*** Know that pledges can be made in cash, stocks, bonds, or other negotiable property. In addition, understand that pledges can be fulfilled over a period of time convenient to the donor and that the full amount of the pledge is not required up front.

8. ***Never, never leave the pledge card!*** If the prospective donor wants to think about it, make an appointment to revisit him or her later but keep the pledge card in your possession. Pledge cards are easily lost, even by people with the best intentions. It can be difficult for the supporter to call the volunteer who visited them and to inform them that they have lost the pledge card. Instead, follow up promptly and set a date to return for the completion of the pledge card.

In a recent campaign, an administrator and a consultant went to visit an influential member of the community at his home. The gentleman had not yet decided on the amount he and his wife would pledge. He said to the administrator, "Leave the card and I will think about it." As the administrator was about to hand over the pledge card, the consultant noticed that he had inadvertently brought the wrong pledge card. He apologized for his error. The gentleman asked about the next step, and the consultant said, "Carefully consider what you will give and you can call me. I will take your word of your pledge and then send you a letter with the card."

When the administrator and consultant got out to the car, the administrator noted that it was fortunate that the consultant had brought the wrong card. The consultant smiled and said, "Sir, after you left cards at the last two visits, I wasn't about to let you do it a third time."

Initially, the administrator was a little surprised that the consultant had intentionally brought the wrong card. However, when the pledges came in for the three visits they had made, the member who called the consultant personally gave a much larger amount than the two members who had kept their pledge cards.

9.   *Complete the pledge card.* Help the prospect to fill out the card. Be certain the total amount is indicated, the payment plan is noted, and the donor has signed the card.

10.   *Thank the donor for his or her time!* All gifts are welcome and accepted graciously, no matter the size. Also, be sure to thank the individual for his or her time even if he or she decides not to make a gift. People must know that their time is valued, whatever the outcome.

In a small nonprofit campaign project in Minnesota, the board president visited an elderly family. The couple pledged $50,000, but the president forgot to have them formally sign the pledge card. Later that evening, the man unexpectedly died, leaving his widow to decide if she would or could now honor the pledge they had made together even though they had not signed the card. Fortunately for the organization, she was still interested in making the commitment.

Asking for the Pledge

You are likely wondering how exactly you should ask for a gift. Many potential donors will ask, "What do you expect from me?" or "What are others giving?" While it can be embarrassing to mention a specific amount, it should not be. If you have thought about it beforehand, your request will be reasonable. If it helps, you may anonymously report what others have pledged or report the average gift. Tell the person that others are responding generously. Contrary to what you may believe, it is a compliment—not an offense—to suggest a specific and substantial amount for someone to carefully consider.

To be tactful and honest, you might say, "For us to reach our goal, each of us must give a considered gift according to our commitment, interest, and financial situation. We hope that you will be among those subscribing x amount per month for three or five years. You may wish to give more, or you may not feel you can give so much. If it is possible for you to consider this amount, your commitment will help us be successful." Tell the prospective donor, "After careful consideration, whatever you decide to give will be appreciated." In my experience, people appreciate this kind of honest and forthright approach. This is not a new idea. The following is a speech given by John D. Rockefeller, Jr. in 1933 to the Citizen Family Welfare Committee of New York City.

I have been asked to say a few words on the techniques of soliciting donations. Perhaps the best way to acquire knowledge of that subject is to ask ourselves the question, "How would I like to be approached for a gift?" The answer, if carefully thought out, may be relied upon as a pretty safe guide to the task of soliciting. I have been brought up to believe, and the conviction only grows on me, that giving ought to be entered into in just the same careful way as investing—that giving is investing, and that it should be tested by the same intelligent standards. Whether we expect dividends in dollars or in human betterment, we need to be sure that the gift or the investment is a wise one and therefore we should know all about it. By the same token, if we are going to other people to interest them in giving to a particular enterprise, we must be able to give them adequate information in regard to it, such information as we would want were we considering a gift.

First of all, then, a solicitor must be well informed in regard to the salient facts about the enterprise for which he is soliciting. Just what is its significance, its importance? How sound is the organization behind it, how well organized? How great is the need? An accurate knowledge of these and similar facts is necessary in order that the solicitor may be able to speak with conviction.

It is a great help to know something about the person whom you are approaching. You cannot deal successfully with all people the same way. Therefore, it is desirable to find out something about the person you are going to—what are his interests, whether you have any friends in common, whether he gave last year, if so how much he gave, what he might be able to give this year, etc. Information such as that puts you more closely in touch with him and makes the approach easier.

Again, one always likes to know what other people are giving. That may be an irrelevant question, but it is an asked question. If I am asked for a contribution, naturally and properly I am influenced in deciding how much I should give by what others are doing.

Another suggestion I like to have made me by a solicitor is how much it is hoped I will give. Of course, such a suggestion can be made in a way that might *be most annoying. I do not like to have anyone tell me what it is my duty to give. There is just one man who is going to decide that question—who has the responsibility of deciding it—and that is myself. But I do like a man to say to me, "We are trying to raise $4,000,000 and are hoping you may be desirous of giving blank dollars. If you see your way clear to do so, it will be an enormous help and encouragement. You may have it in mind to give more; if so, we shall be glad. On the other hand, you may feel you cannot give as much in view of other responsibilities. If that is the case, we shall understand. Whatever you give after thinking the matter over carefully in the light of the need, your other obligations, and your desire to do your full share as a citizen, will be gratefully received and deeply appreciated." When you talk to a man like that he is glad to meet you again and will not take the other elevator when he sees you in the corridor because you backed him to the wall and forced him to give.*

Of supreme importance is it to make a pleasant, friendly contact with the prospective giver. Some people have a less keen sense of their duty and responsibility than others do. With them, a little urging may be helpful. But with most people, a convincing presentation of the facts and the need is far more effective. When a solicitor comes to you and lays on your heart the responsibility that rests so heavily on his; when his earnestness gives convincing evidence of how seriously interested he is; when he makes it clear that he knows you are no less anxious to do your duty in the matter than he is, that you are just as conscientious, that he feels sure all you need is realize the importance of the enterprise, and if so, how much, it is for him alone to decide.

To recap then, briefly: know your subject; be so sold on it yourself that you can convincingly present its claims in the fewest possible words. A letter may well precede an interview, but personal contact is the most effective. Know as much as you can about the man to whom you go; give him a general idea as to the contributions being made by others in his group, and suggest in a gracious and tactful way what you would be glad to have him give, leaving it solely to him to decide what he shall give. Be kindly and considerate. Thus will you get closest to a man's heart and his pocketbook.

A Capital Campaign victory can be lost by

- Indifference
- Procrastination
- The use of letters, telephone calls, or chance meetings rather than planned and scheduled personal visits
- Thinking "our organization's circumstances are different" as a basis for circumventing proven campaign methods
- A failure to see the value of the campaign
- A failure to become aligned with the vision, or a tendency toward disinterestedness
- A failure to develop a belief in the ultimate achievability of the objectives

A Capital Campaign victory can be achieved by

- Seeing that all of the nonprofit's supporters attend the kick-off celebration
- Strict adherence to the time schedule
- Advance visits with organizational leaders, other influential community leaders, and those business leaders who have more resources and are capable of making larger gifts
- A well-organized, informed, and enthusiastic group of visitors
- Personal visits with every member of the nonprofit's community
- Regular report meetings attended by each visitor
- The recognition that capital needs are different from annual pledging and require a thoughtful and inspirational effort on the part of each member of the community, leader, and follower alike

The following chapters will cover each of the phases of the campaign in detail: the Advance Gift Phase, the Kick-off Event, the Pattern Gift Phase, and the Victory Team Phase.

MAIN MESSAGE

Personal visitation creates and enhances community and organizational spirit. Treat people with honesty and respect. Let them know what is required to reach a particular goal. Finally, always ask a prospective donor for a specific gift in person.

CHAPTER 8

Campaign Phase I:
Leadership Giving and Advance Gifts

A nonprofit board member once told me, "I learned a long time ago not to decide what others are not going to do." That statement has stayed with me and has given me the strength to ask people for things that I otherwise might not. I try to remember that it is always a good idea to assume the best of people and let them prove you right.

While all phases of the campaign are critical, this particular phase will be predictive of what you are going to raise during the entire course of your capital campaign. Sometimes we also call this phase the *goal confirmation phase*. This phase happens quickly and quietly and is conducted by the campaign steering committee (executive committee) and authorized by the nonprofit board and administrators. This part of your campaign is nonpublic and it happens after your feasibility study but before your kick-off event. The pledges you raise during this period of your campaign typically represent 50 percent of the total funds you will raise during the entire campaign. Even if your organization has needs requiring $10 million, if you only raise $3 million during this phase of the campaign, you should announce that your goal is $6 million. Some firms call this phase the *challenge gift phase*, but I do not like to use that terminology, because it implies that there are gifts that are not challenging. In fact, we believe in equal sacrifice, and we believe that all gifts, regardless of amount, are equally challenging to secure.

Somewhat conversely, the advance gift phase should not begin with an official stated campaign goal but should begin instead with a statement of your campaign needs. This distinction is very important for people to understand. The needs of your organization or nonprofit institution were established in the case statement. However, if you are not able to raise this amount, you should not state it as your goal. If you do, you will be setting yourself up for disappointment. Until you determine what is raised during the advance gifts phase, you should not set your goal. Establishing a goal based on hard numbers is much better and much easier to justify.

Now is the time to begin asking for pledges, using the format outlined in the last chapter and remembering that a personal touch matters. You should begin with those closest to the campaign, including the campaign leadership. The campaign leadership was selected based on their need to make an inspirational gift. Now, beginning with the organization's administrator, they should be called upon to make their pledge. Before they begin asking any other members of the community to make pledges, all of the campaign leadership should make pledges of their own.

Once your campaign leaders have made their pledges, your consultant will work with you to help you identify other perceived leaders or affluent members of the community who will likely make large donations. During the advance gifts phase, your volunteers will typically visit 10 to 15 percent of the business and community leaders. The most effective method is to begin with those closest to the campaign and to expand the circle outward from there. Most other fundraising firms will tell you to begin your visits with the wealthiest potential donors first. However, by visiting with those closest to the campaign first instead of jumping right into asking the wealthiest prospective donors for commitments, you will generate enthusiasm for the campaign and make it easier for those leaders to recruit others to their committees.

It is important to emphasize quality giving during this early period, since the pattern of giving set at this stage will influence all other gifts secured during the course of the campaign.

An administrator involved in a campaign for $5 million told me that there was no one on their list of prospective donors that could give a lead gift of 10 percent. I argued and said that someone must have the ability to make that commitment over a five-year period, but he remained firm; he did not want to give me a name. Finally, I asked who the wealthiest person was on their list of prospective donors, and he gave me a name. I arranged a meeting between the administrator and with this individual and told the administrator that even if he was right that the person was not able to commit to such a large gift, he needed to ask in order for the campaign to be a success. The administrator was extremely nervous about going to the meeting; he was worried that he was going to insult this very wealthy man. A few minutes into the meeting, the administrator blurted out that he really needed a $500,000 gift to make the campaign a success. The businessman considered for a moment and said, "I would be honored to make that pledge." The administrator was stunned but left the meeting with a changed mind. He became a big advocate of asking for the lead pledge.

It is important to evaluate your progress frequently—at least weekly—and to include a measurement of readiness of response, spirit of endorsement, level of cooperation, and actual commitments of top gifts. Because the nature of the contributions is confidential, your consultant should prepare and present this report to the committee.

After the advance gifts phase, you will be able to see progress toward your goal, and all of the options are open to you. The steering committee will confirm the official campaign goal or, if necessary, adjust the objective to the appropriate level based on what you were able to raise during the advance gifts phase. Once you have established and confirmed your goal, you will present it to your entire organizational community at the kick-off event.

When a nonprofit community works together to achieve a common goal, that is as important as whatever funds are raised during the campaign. In twenty years, the organization might not remember how much money was raised or what it was used for, but those who worked together toward the achievement of a common goal will remember if they conducted a successful campaign.

The amount pledged during the advance gifts phase provides the basis for the campaign objective announced at the kick-off event. The event itself is fun and is used as both a social event and to share information with the community. All prospective donors, supporters, and families of those involved in the organization are encouraged to attend, and no solicitations of gifts take place. It is important that everyone is put at ease and people know that at this event, they will not be asked to make a pledge.

Naming Opportunities

I was consulting for a campaign in Maryland that aimed to raise $4 million. Part of the needs of the campaign were several renovated meeting rooms. The building committee chair proposed that each room naming opportunity should have a $25,000 gift associated with it. Given the scale of gifts needed to reach the goal, I suggested that perhaps a $100,000 gift amount would be more appropriate. She resisted until I convinced her not only that we needed the higher scale of gifts to reach our goal but that there were going to be many people in the community who could give $5,000 a year for five years. Unless we were going to give all of those people a naming opportunity, it would not be fair and could cause hard feelings. We did not have an endless supply of meeting rooms with naming rights, so it made sense to raise the gift amount for the room naming opportunities.

People often ask me for my thoughts regarding memorial gifts and naming opportunities. I feel that memorial gifts or donations made in memory or gratitude of someone who has passed are a wonderful way to contribute to a campaign. Whether it is a gift to a church building fund, the community hospital, Boys and Girls Club, local library, or school auditorium, all are worthy causes, and a gift made in memory of a loved one is a wonderful gesture. As far as naming opportunities are concerned, I believe that naming opportunities for a nonprofit campaign need to fit with the personality and mission of the organization. I have visited some organizations that have small brass plaques on everything from windows to the janitor's closet. However, there are some nonprofits that resist recognizing donors altogether in the form of brass plates or plaques because they want the focus to remain on the organization as a whole and not on individuals. However, naming opportunities have encouraged many, many people to contribute vast amounts of money over the years, and so I would certainly not rule it out. That said, I have some advice when the decision is made to offer naming opportunities: Make sure there are enough opportunities for a large number of families. You might be surprised at how many people or families will express an interest in having their name on something. People like being connected to an organization and an institution they support, and receiving recognition for their support is very appealing to many people. Nevertheless, if you will allow someone's name on a room, for instance, make certain you allow this for all rooms, not just some of the rooms. You can offer naming opportunities for conference rooms, playing fields, benches, or an auditorium. By offering more opportunities for naming rights, you can keep the dollar amounts lower; when your naming opportunities are limited, you must set the dollar amounts high.

During a project several years ago with a nonprofit, I was working with an administrator so dedicated to the cause and consumed by the success of his school organization that he made the building of a new auditorium theater one of the most important objectives of his career. He believed that he had been called to provide for future generations and members of the community of students and families. During a campaign visit with a successful businessman, the administrator and I asked him to thoughtfully consider becoming the lead gift donor with a donation of $1 million. We knew that this lead gift would ensure a successful campaign. Along with it, the naming rights for the new auditorium theater would also be available. The prospective donor thought about his gift and confessed that he truly felt that he was blessed to have such resources at his disposal. He explained that he felt he was merely a custodian of the resources and that he felt it was his job to be a good steward and to give to others. This meeting was emotional and heartfelt, and the donor eventually accepted the challenge for the lead gift of $1 million. However, he declined to have the auditorium theater named after him. He said it would not be appropriate to put his name on the new facility because he felt that the cause was greater than one man. I was awed to be in the presence of such a great man. How could this get any better? Several months later, after the campaign had come to a very successful end, we arranged a groundbreaking ceremony for the new auditorium theater. During the ceremony, an announcement was made that the lead gift donor had ultimately accepted the naming opportunity but he was not going to use his own name. Instead, he wanted to name the new auditorium theater after the administrator who had worked tirelessly to make the campaign a success. I still get tears in my eyes when I think of that day.

Some nonprofits want to set a goal shortly after the first few gifts are in. It is only natural. You will be excited, and you will want to set your sights high. However, our recommendation is to wait until the last minute before the kick-off event to decide on your goal, based on what has been pledged to date. This encourages everyone to continue working until the last minute. If the goal is set too early, people tend to slow down.

By holding off, you encourage them to work as hard as possible for as long as possible and you lay the foundation for an extremely successful campaign.

MAIN MESSAGE

Set an official campaign goal only after key leaders and large potential donors make their financial commitments to the total cost of the project. It is important for these donors to make commitments based on actual needs rather than an arbitrary goal. That way, when you set your goal, you will be basing it on current performance and funds you have already raised. In addition, use naming opportunities only if this fits with the needs and personality of your organization

CHAPTER 9
The Campaign Kick-off Event

At a recent campaign kick-off event for a small local nonprofit, a man and his wife arrived together. Though they had not discussed the campaign with each other, they both fully expected to be asked for a pledge before the end of the evening. They assumed this, even though the invitation explicitly stated that there would be no solicitation of funds. As they sat down, and the testimonials from students and teachers began, the man leaned over to his wife and quietly told her that they could contribute $10,000 when the pledge cards were distributed. She nodded in agreement. As they continued to listen to members of the community talk about the importance of the needs, the man leaned over again and said, "On second thought, when they pass out the pledge cards, we can do $25,000." Again, she agreed. The board president gave her closing remarks, and the members who had attended dispersed and said their goodbyes. The man and his wife drove home, amazed at the event. A few days later when the campaign volunteer met with the couple, the woman said that since the kick-off event, they had done a great deal of careful thinking and consideration and had ultimately committed to a $100,000 pledge, ten times what they thought their initial commitment would be.

Each time I hear a story like this, it reinforces my belief that the kick-off event is not the proper venue in which to ask people for their gift. Time and time again I have seen this to be the case. There are two reasons for this. In some cases, the testimonials from participants, members, and administrators are so moving that people may find themselves committing to a gift they cannot afford. Other times, they may feel pressured to make a large donation in a setting where everyone around them is signing a pledge card. The second reason that I feel that the kick-off event is not the proper venue to ask for funds is that some people will not put a great deal of thought into their gift, and instead they will choose a token amount without being truly challenged. In a group setting, you run the risk of people conferring with each other to decide what the average gift should be. That is not what you want.

It is reasonable that you might ask, if we do not request pledges at the kick-off event, what is the point of holding one? However, there are three important objectives to the kick-off event. The first is to educate supporters about the feasibility study and what the campaign committee decided regarding the needs and the proposed solutions. In order to do this, it is important to provide a clear case statement that was developed by your consultant from the results of the feasibility study. The case statement should be delivered by the campaign chair. The second objective for the kick-off event is to introduce and recognize all of those members who are involved in the campaign. These people are the face of your campaign, and your nonprofit's community will be meeting with them—hopefully in person—over the coming months. The kick-off event is a great time to put faces to names. Finally, the third objective of the event is to announce how much money has been pledged thus far. If you have set your goal already based on the pledges to date, you should also announce that at this time. However, remember that if you decide to announce your campaign goal at the event, you should have at least half of the goal pledged already.

Many years ago, my wife and I were invited to a kick-off event. It was a school in a community we had lived in, and we felt a personal connection to both the organization and the community. We had driven in from out of town to attend the kick-off event. Because the event was to take place in the late afternoon at a beautiful downtown hotel, we both assumed that the event would include a sit-down dinner. Neither my wife nor I had eaten, but when we arrived, we found only a small hors d'oeuvres table set up in one corner with an open bar in another corner. We were told that we were each welcome to eat five hors d'oeuvres and have two drinks. Given the advanced age of the attendees and the lack of chairs, we did not want to take up two seats. The program lacked a formal explanation for why the event was happening, other than the fact that the organization was looking to raise funds to expand. Renderings of the proposed expansion were hidden in a corner. The program was disjointed, and the rhythm of the testimonials was interrupted by seemingly random musical entertainment. The people chosen to speak on behalf of the program did not effectively make the case and certainly were not practiced. My wife and I left the event wondering what the needs of the organization truly were, as we were never explicitly told. Later that night at dinner, instead of discussing the needs of the organization and how we would support them, my wife and I focused on how poorly the message of the campaign had been delivered. We were certain that no one who had been in attendance had taken away any more from the event than we had. This experience only served to reinforce my belief that an effective capital campaign kick-off event should be focused and fun for the attendees, and everyone should come away from the event feeling inspired and motivated.

My company has been involved in all types of kick-off events at a variety of venues, from elaborate country clubs to modest fellowship halls. Regardless of where your event is held, it needs to build community and reflect the personality of your organization. I have always been a strong advocate of a sit-down meal with an organized program because it provides a relaxed atmosphere while allowing attendees to socialize with eight to ten people at once, which can go a long way toward building enthusiasm for a project. I have also found it helpful if the members of the organization are not directly involved in serving the food and cleaning up, because it is much more effective if they are involved in the event and they spend their time and energy paying attention to and engaging the guests. Once again, a personal touch is important.

The purpose of the kick-off event is to educate, inspire, and celebrate what has been accomplished thus far. If you keep that in mind and ensure that all of your volunteers are in the proper frame of mine, your event will be successful.

The importance of the kick-off event cannot be overstated. It is one of the most important elements of the entire plan of campaign. While most kick-off events revolve around a dinner, many of our nonprofit clients have chosen to host a brunch or a barbecue instead, in keeping with the personality of their organization. The only thing that matters when choosing a venue is that it must be able to accommodate all invited members. It must also be free of charge and have an adequate sound system so that the news about the campaign can be delivered.

As with any event where an accurate head count is important, you should mail an invitation with an RSVP card several weeks ahead of time. The best way to do this is to hand-address and mail the invitations first class. A considerate nonprofit campaign committee will ensure that the RSVP cards are stamped so that attendees do not have to search for a stamp or pay additional postage. You want to make sure that responding is as easy as possible for your invited guests. Even under the best circumstances, a great deal of advertising and follow-up are necessary to get the desired attendance. In most cases, the nonprofit will advertise the event in the organization's newsletter and announce it at board meetings. Additionally, nonprofits can use email or the organization's website to announce the event. In some cases, you can even recruit volunteers to phone community members and encourage them to attend the event.

The invitation itself should be formal and should include the date, location, and purpose of the event. It should also announce the keynote speaker and should clearly indicate that there will be no solicitation of pledges at the event. An organization that wants to have a successful campaign kick-off event should do everything in its power to get the greatest number of individuals to attend.

By this point, your kick-off event committee chair should have recruited his or her committee, which has been very busy planning the event. They should have considered the venue, the time of day, the menu, the anticipated attendance, a list of potential keynote speakers, whether or not childcare will be needed during the event, transportation for those attendees who cannot drive, parking, name tags, event brochures, etc. Obviously, there are a great many things to consider!

The program for the kick-off event is essential. It lets everyone know what to expect and roughly how long the event will last. A sample event program should detail the following:

- Welcome
- Opening remarks
- Dinner (forty minutes) or other social time
- Presentation of the overview/purpose of the campaign
- Acknowledgment and recognition of volunteers
- Testimonials
- Introduction of the keynote speaker
- Progress of Campaign

- Announce the Campaign goal
- Inspirational words by administrator
- Closing remarks

It is important to keep the event on time and on topic. If it lasts more than two hours, you will begin to lose people—both their attention and their attendance, as many people cannot commit to a long event. You want your attendees to leave feeling inspired, not drained.

The program should provide a brief presentation of the total needs of the campaign. It is also important to walk through the plans and the scope of the project so that the attendees have an idea of the end goals. All supporters who have agreed to take on leadership roles in the campaign should be recognized by name. Interspersed throughout the program, it is important to include testimonials given by various nonprofit leaders who can talk about the importance of the organization in their lives and what the organization means to the community. These testimonials are essentially endorsements of the proposed plans with a personal emphasis, and they are extremely effective. The people selected to give these testimonials should be a good cross-section of the organization's community, from instructors to administrators to alumni from business and community leaders to supporters to board members.

Some organizations will also have entertainment before or after the presentation or during the dinner. If you are raising money for a music program, a musical performance would be a good idea. Here are a few points to consider:

Let the attendees write their own names on name tags. By doing this, you will be sure to call attendees by the name they prefer. For example, while you may have an attendee whose name is Michael, he may prefer to be called Mike. If he is allowed to write his own name tag, people will be sure to call him Mike. Additionally, if you pre-print all of the name tags and there is poor turn-out, the absence of the other members will be obvious from the sea of unclaimed name tags on the welcome table.

If you decide to have a keynote speaker at your kick-off event, remember that his or her job is to inspire attendees and to act as a draw for community members. Good choices for keynote speakers could be the organization's founder, a business or an award-winning community leader instructor, or a successful alumnus supporter.

For those organizations that are trying to raise money for an auditorium or a theater, it is often helpful to the cause to hold the event in a local theater that is similar to the one you are trying to build. It will contribute to the vision.

During one kick-off event for an organization held at a banquet facility, one of the campaign leaders brought out a roll of construction tape during dinner and ran it a third of the way through the audience. She announced that what she had just measured off was the size of the current theater. Then she pointed to all the attendees sitting beyond the mark and said that if the event had been held in the current theater, none of them could have attended. It was a very effective way to drive home the need to expand the facility.

If there is a way to skillfully include the current organization participants in your kick-off event, you will have a better chance of getting their family and friends to attend. Of course, if the children involved are young, the parents may be distracted for the rest of the event. This is where a consideration of childcare may be important.

There are differing opinions about the proper timing for distributing the campaign brochure, described in Chapter 6. Some people argue that the brochure should not be given out during the kick-off event because people will be focused on reading it and will not pay attention to the program. Others will argue that the brochure should be given to people as they leave the event; that way they will have the necessary information but will not be distracted by it during the presentations and testimonials. There are still others who argue that the delivery of the brochure provides a good reason to make personal visits to members of the community during the coming days and weeks.

I have been at events where the brochure has been passed out at the kick-off event, and I have seen cases where the brochure is given during a personal visit. Neither method has cost a campaign success or ensured a victory. However, it is always important that the campaign fits the personality of the organization and leaders of the effort.

MAIN MESSAGE

The purpose of the kick-off event is to educate and inspire all members of the community. It is not a time to ask for pledges. Do not charge for the event. Often, a campaign kick-off event is the only time the entire nonprofit community gets together for one individual event. Therefore, it is important to make it enjoyable and memorable.

CHAPTER 10

Campaign Phases 2 and 3:
Pattern Gifts and Victory Teams

At this point, you have held your kick-off event and your community knows you are well on your way to achieving your goal. You have now reached what is officially considered the start of the campaign's public phase. Because you should have at least half of your goal pledged prior to the kick-off event, you will now begin to raise the remaining half of your goal. This phase consists of two parts: the first phase is called the *pattern gifts phase* and the second phase is the *victory teams phase*. Both phases have similar administrative responsibilities, but they differ in terms of the size of the volunteer effort and the asking amounts. During the pattern gifts phase, you will still be targeting relatively large gifts and donations, while during the victory teams phase, you will be visiting individuals with more modest means. This phase of the campaign includes all remaining prospective donors that have not yet been called upon.

Pattern Gifts: The financial goal of the Pattern Gifts Phase is to raise 30 percent of the total goal. During the review of the scale of gifts, you identified which members of the community you would visit during the pattern gifts phase. The average pledge amount you are requesting will vary based on your total goal. Once the kick-off event ends, those campaign visitors tasked with requesting gifts during this phase should be ready to go. What that means is that just prior to the kick-off event, they should be called upon to make their pledges, and they should be trained to solicit gifts. Remember that no one should be asked to make a pledge by someone who has not already done so themselves. Likewise, once someone is asked and makes his or her pledge, he or she is eligible to become a visitor and to ask others for their pledges. There is a great deal of potential during this phase, but there are also opportunities for traps and mistakes. Having a consultant present to oversee the training and debrief the visitors is essential. It is also essential to break bad habits early.

This phase is where you will realize the true value of the feasibility study. You will likely find that during the feasibility study, many people noted on their questionnaires that they would be willing to participate. Therefore, you already have a list of people who want to help. Imagine how difficult things would be if you reached this phase without knowing who wanted to help and you had to spend your time cold-calling everyone in the community to ask about their willingness to help.

The pattern gifts chair meets with the consultant and reports as needed. The consultant continues to oversee the training of volunteers. The pattern gifts chair also reports weekly to the campaign chair and the organization's administrator.

You will have a relatively small number of visitors, but they will have a great deal of responsibility. It is imperative that you treat all members of the community with the same respect and that you use the "ask" technique described in Chapter 6. Anyone who accepts the invitation to become a visitor will receive orientation and coaching sessions. The first meeting will be an initial orientation meeting, which includes the first coaching session (we coach volunteers constantly throughout the campaign) and pledge card selection. That meeting will be followed by regular report meetings. Pledge card selection is an important element in an effective and successful effort. It is important to allow campaign visitors to select whom they wish to call on rather than to assign cards to them, because visitors will feel more comfortable asking for pledges if they are comfortable with the people they are visiting. My firm allows visitors to choose the number of visits they wish to make and the individuals or families they visit. Other firms assign pledge cards based on geographic area or some other means, and I wonder why they do not let the visitors make the decisions for themselves. Even if campaign volunteers are excited about the campaign, they may also be reluctant to make specific visits out of fear of rejection or because of some other concern. Therefore, you should make it as easy as possible for your volunteers to make the campaign effort a success. Allow them to decide whom they will visit.

Finally, during this time you will also complete the recruitment and training for the final phase of pledge solicitation: the Victory Teams.

Victory Teams: The goal of this phase is to raise the final 20 percent of the campaign goal. This is an intense period of the campaign because during this phase, the most visitors will be trained in order to reach out to all of the members of the community who have not yet been visited. To accomplish this, it is absolutely crucial to have accurate enrollment and community records.

During this phase, our consultant will continue to provide a brief weekly report to all appropriate leaders, as well as our office. We want to make sure that you are on target to reach your goal.

As with all efforts, committee members can get tired and feel burnt out towards the end of the campaign. It is at this point that it may become necessary to use extraordinary means to get your volunteers to refocus their efforts.

One of the very first campaigns on which I worked was approximately $50,000 short of our goal as we neared the end of the ten-week campaign. With the Executive Director preparing to visit on Victory Sunday and the number of remaining calls dwindling, I spoke to the committee about the slowdown. At one of our final meetings, I wrote a memo and prepared it for the campaign steering committee members' signatures. The memo stated that if they did not raise the remaining funds by a certain date, they would collectively contribute the additional funds. They all reluctantly signed the letter without exception. The finance chair astutely said, "This is just our consultant's way of telling us to keep our eye on the ball and get our calls done." Within days, the goal was reached and I received an envelope containing torn-up pieces of the memo. I was very pleased.

If new prospective donors are identified during either of these phases, they should be approached not because you are desperate but because they have been identified as potential supporters and deserve to be treated like everyone else. Some committee members may not want to offend newcomers by asking for money just as they join the community, but in my experience, asking people to become a part of the future of the organization by making a contribution to the campaign makes them feel included; it does not offend them.

During a campaign in Arkansas, a mother had recently moved into the community and become part of the organization and enrolled her children at the school. Some committee members did not want to approach her for a pledge for fear of offending her due to her short tenure in the community. However, as we were still in the midst of the project, I encouraged the committee to approach her. We argued over the asking amount, as no one knew her well. Eventually, we decided to ask her for a pledge of $25,000. The pledge card was made up and the campaign chairman prepped to visit the woman. When he arrived, he was pleased with her enthusiasm for the campaign and the fact that she was happy to be a part of the future of the organization. During their visit, the woman shared a great deal of information with the campaign chairman about her positive financial situation. It was obvious she had great means and could consider a gift greater than $25,000. After the visit, the chairman called me to report that he respectfully asked her to consider a gift of $75,000, which she cheerfully pledged.

Victory Celebration

The Victory Celebration is an especially important event. It says "thank you" in a memorable way and marks the completion of the more active phase of the campaign. However, the victory celebration does not necessarily mean that your consultant will be departing, especially if significant outstanding calls remain. The celebration should take place in anticipation of reaching of the pledge goal, not simply to mark the end of the campaign. Some organizations invite the surrounding community to the event, particularly if a building project is planned, as they know their future building plans will be an inconvenience to the community. The victory celebration might also be coupled with an upcoming event in the organization's history, such as a twenty-five-year celebration. As with all aspects of the campaign, the victory celebration must reflect the personality of the organization. It should be organized in a similar fashion to the kick-off event, with attention paid to recognizing the hard work of all who contributed to the work of the campaign.

MAIN MESSAGE

If you have done your Feasibility Study correctly, you will be able to readily identify your workers for the pattern gifts and Victory Teams phases of the campaign. Follow-through in these phases is the key to the ultimate success of the campaign. Recognition of the hard work done throughout the campaign is needed to boost morale and motivate those who will need to continue to monitor the campaign.

CHAPTER 11
Follow-Through: Keeping the Campaign Alive

At the conclusion of our firm's contracted resident service, all records and documents pertaining to the campaign belong to your organization and are left for your reference and records. Everything belongs to you, and you will have all files to reference in the future. Based upon past experience and our knowledge of your particular campaign, our director will design an effective collection and follow-up program for you. These plans assure minimum pledge loss and will help to maintain the interest and support of the many volunteers who gave their time and energy to the campaign. We will maintain contact with the leaders of your organization throughout the pledge payment period and be available to answer any questions they may have.

There are two main objectives for this period of the campaign. The first is to keep the campaign in front of the community as a reminder that it is still going on while they continue to pay their pledges. The second goal is to continue visiting new prospective donors to the community to gain their support for the project.

I am frequently asked how much of the actual pledges are paid over the three-to-five-year period, and I always say that, as with every other part of the campaign, that is up to you. Historically, approximately 96 percent of pledges are paid. We are now seeing that organizations with an excellent follow-up committee may see a substantial increase in pledges by continuing to approach new prospective donors and call on them to join in the campaign, even after the campaign has been completed.

> At a nonprofit in Maryland, two years after the official campaign had ended, a young couple moved to the community and began to take advantage of the organization. The follow-up committee called on them regarding the campaign. Although they were new to the community, they felt that the project was very worthwhile, and they had seen the transformation of the organization, which is why they chose to become members. They pledged $400,000.

Follow-through works when there is a committed team assigned to the committee. It is impossible for any program to sustain its momentum for thirty-six to sixty months without constant assistance. Your job is to keep the momentum for the campaign alive over the course of the commitment period. Afterwards, the follow-up committee should meet at least once a quarter. The publicity representative needs to meet with the campaign treasurer and organization's secretary at least monthly to gather information that can be used in the newsletter, updates, and special mailings.

To have the most effective Follow-Up Program:

1. Appoint a small ad hoc committee of three to five dedicated individuals who have displayed leadership during the course of the campaign to oversee the follow-through on pledge payments.

2. Keep all campaign records, collection procedures, and accounts completely separate from other expense and income records to minimize confusion

3. Treat all gifts, payments, and records confidentially.

4. Have the financial secretary keep a record of pledge payments and send reminders to donors one month before their payments are due. This person should also provide a list of delinquent payments for the follow-through task force.

5. Keep accurate records of giving and use money only for the purposes listed in the campaign.

6. Make positive announcements to keep volunteers and friends of the organization informed and encouraged.

7. Write positive and personal thank you letters. Never write negative letters or letters pressuring donors.

8. Enlist new donors through personal visitation.

9.   Some contributors have made one-year or cash gifts. Often, these people will consider additional gifts in subsequent years if they are approached properly and in person.

Some helpful things to keep the campaign alive:

1.   Newsletters and Updates

At the end of each three-month period, it is helpful to mail an informative letter, progress report, or newsletter to donors, updating them on the results of the pledges and the progress of the campaign to date. You should also explain your future plans. Communication is one of the most effective means of maintaining momentum. When major projects are completed, you should try to obtain coverage from both the organization and local media outlets. It is incredibly gratifying for both donors and volunteers to see the progress of the campaign reported on in the media.

2.   Frequent Announcements

Make frequent announcements to various meetings and gatherings at your organization, including board meetings. Remember that people are drawn to organizations that are vibrant and alive, where there is a good energy, and where worthwhile things are happening. Make sure that visitors are aware that the organization has recently undertaken a *successful* campaign. Announce when important milestones have been reached.

In Case of Delinquent Payments

Each case should be handled according to its own specific circumstances. If a personal call becomes necessary, the visitor should position himself or herself as a friend interested in helping another find a solution to a situation. Do not use the mail except for quarterly or annual statements. Make sure to always call or visit in person to avoid any misunderstandings.

In the rare case that it becomes obvious the pledge will never be redeemed, offer to reduce or revise the initial amount pledged. If this does not solve the problem, offer to recommend to the committee that the pledge be canceled. It is useless to keep harassing someone who cannot or will not fulfill his or her obligation. It will only cause hard feelings, and that was not the spirit in which the campaign was conducted.

Additionally, someone who may have initially committed to a pledge in good faith may have undergone financial hardship or another situation which makes fulfilling the pledge difficult. Harping on someone's inability to pay will only induce negative feelings.

There may be setbacks when collecting pledges, but negativity must not be allowed to detract from a general tone of optimism, sincerity, and urgency. If the campaign leaders reflect any doubts or misgivings about the good faith of those who have pledged, you will adversely affect collections; the negative feelings will spread. Nevertheless, if you constantly confirm your belief that the program will proceed as planned based on your faith in the pledges and the community members, the positivity will spread as well. Each pledge should be regarded as a solemn commitment upon which you are building the future of your nonprofit organization.

Helpful Tools

To make sure that you have the most accurate records, match the computer records of pledges to the original signed pledge cards. You should also keep these files on electronic backup somewhere off site so that in the event of an emergency, your records will be safe.

You should also make sure to leave sample kits containing all the materials you used in the office. The kits should contain the names of the people who demonstrated leadership of one kind or another during the campaign. As time passes, you will find it interesting to see how the organization progressed and achieved a successful campaign. The plan of campaign will always be a good resource to consider for any future campaigns.

Nominations for Campaign Follow-Up Committee

Duties: Publicity, monitoring of pledges, following up delinquencies, financial projections, and tracking and convening.

MAIN MESSAGE

Keep the campaign in front of the community and show them progress. Campaign follow-up procedures are necessary, and the volunteers who serve on this committee have a great responsibility to keep the campaign alive.

CHAPTER 12
Combining Annual with Capital Campaigns

Over the past several years, many organizations have approached me about the possibility of combining the annual campaign with a capital campaign. While this used to be an all but forbidden practice in fundraising circles, my firm has worked very hard to establish a track record of success in combining these efforts. The key to being successful with this combined effort is making sure that you clearly delineate the objectives of each program and educate the community about the mission of each. There can be an advantage to combining these fundraising efforts: there is less stress on your volunteers, and it is easier for you to define the objectives of each campaign.

Organizational members are often confused about the differences between the two campaign efforts. It is not uncommon to hear supporters ask, "Didn't we just donate to the organization last year?" Supporters can become confused about the difference between annual campaigns, which include elements of the annual budget, and capital needs such as new construction, renovation, or property acquisition.

Capital campaigns usually raise funds for permanent properties in amounts that are so significant that the annual budget of the organization could not possibly address these costs. I have found that there are some supporters who understand the difference very well. There are often times when supporters who have historically given small amounts during annual giving will surprise the nonprofit administration and pledge large sums when a naming opportunity for an auditorium or a playing field is available. This may be because the person feels that it is more important to contribute to a lasting part of the organization—something that has an opportunity to become part of the organization's legacy—than to contribute to administrative costs. It could be that contributing to paying the nonprofit's utilities or buying software for the office's computers does not excite him or her, but playing a large role in the future of the organization does. Whatever the reason, it is crucial that leaders of the community and administration do a better job explaining to our supporters what it costs to provide the necessary opportunities and activities that are so vital to the organization on an annual basis. There are many nonprofits that would greatly benefit from a consolidated effort to educate and encourage financial support for annual purposes in their organizations. The challenge is therefore to differentiate the specific objectives of each campaign for the community.

When you are deciding the timing of your capital campaign, the real concern should be the urgency of your needs, not the timing of the annual campaign. Today, nearly half of the projects in which my firm is involved conduct both the annual and capital campaign simultaneously. The basic tenets of the campaign strategy remain the same: every visit should be conducted personally and respectfully, and every visit should educate the community on the different goals supported by each campaign.

In order to help make this clear to the community, I've found it useful to have two different pledge cards, one for the annual campaign and one for the capital campaign. The cards should be printed in different colors to further distinguish between the two. When approaching the prospective donor, the request for a pledge should at least revolve around maintaining current annual giving levels while reaching for the longer-term pledge for the capital effort—which is usually three to five years.

My firm has helped nonprofit clients achieve great results by conducting joint campaigns. Even while requesting that supporters simply maintain their current levels of giving to the annual campaign, we usually experience a 5 percent to 10 percent increase (sometimes higher) in total pledges to the annual campaign. This may be due to one of two important factors. First, all requests are made in person to supporters who are asked to thoughtfully consider the giving by their peers. Second, our method includes all members of your constituency. Because of this, we will always generate a greater number of donors participating and pledging to the annual campaign; no one is left out or overlooked. Additionally, our capital campaigns continue to generate above-average achievement. Although part-time firms will challenge our results and tell their clients that such success is impossible (because they cannot achieve similar results), our clients are more than happy to discuss our method and the success they were able to achieve by working with us. The secret to successful campaigns is simple: full-time, on-site direction of all aspects of the campaign coupled with a highly ethical approach.

Recently, I went to a meeting at a nonprofit at which I had done a project several years ago. The board president stood up and said, "When I last met with Jim, he told me that annual pledges typically do not increase during the pledging period." He then said, "Well, he was wrong. We saw a 10 percent increase in annual giving during the first year of the campaign."

There are advantages and disadvantages of conducting the annual and capital campaigns at the same time. The following advantages and disadvantages have been reported to me over the years by administrators who have tried this approach with other fundraising consulting firms.

Advantages

1. The campaign is usually conducted in the fall, the traditional time for fundraising.
2. Those interested in the annual campaign will be more apt to support a Capital Campaign.
3. Combining campaigns maximizes the volunteers' time and effort.
4. The community will become acquainted with a visitation program that is high quality and involves every supporter. This will be of value in future fundraising efforts.

Disadvantages

1. If the campaigns are not conducted properly or you do not have a consultant available to monitor both campaigns simultaneously, one cause may hurt the other.

2. If not done properly, it is difficult to get any significant increase in the annual pledging during the period of the Capital Campaign.

3. You may conduct appraisals for the capital gift pledge but not for the annual budget.

While our firm enjoys all of the advantages of combining the two campaigns, the method we employ does not experience any of the disadvantages. If a dual campaign is determined to be in the best interest of the client, there are some things that will improve the campaign's chances of success and there are some things that should be avoided.

Things to Do

1. Use separate pledge cards and make them different colors. The annual budget card should be for one year, and the Capital Campaign card should be for three years or more.

2. The case for both elements of the campaign must be very clear and well presented, both in print and in person.

3. Resist any effort to reduce giving to the annual campaign in order to give to the Capital Campaign or vice versa. Do not take from one to give to the other.

4. Emphasize the proper relationship between the two campaigns. Generally, the annual budget is basic, while the Capital Campaign consists of "over and above" giving.

5. Have the board president or administrator emphasize the difference between annual development and fundraising.

6. Develop a comprehensive training program for volunteers and everyone working on the campaign.

7. Gather as much information as possible about current pledges and pledging families.

Things to Avoid

1. Do not allow or encourage competition between the goals of the annual budget and the capital needs. The annual budget is necessary to provide for the most vital programs and opportunities offered by the organization.
2. Do not campaign for any significant increase in the annual budget.
3. Do not allow a combined goal with certain percentages to be specified for each of the two elements.

MAIN MESSAGE

The needs of the organization are more important than trying to "time" the campaign. Capital Campaigns should never adversely affect Annual Campaigns.

CHAPTER 13
Selecting the Right Consulting Firm

When nonprofit leaders decide it is time to embark on a capital campaign, one of the first questions should be whether or not to use an outside consultant. Those who have been involved in a major capital campaign without the service of an outside consultant can attest to how difficult it is to conduct a campaign in addition to all of their regular duties. Those who conduct the campaign on their own tend to raise significantly less than when using an outside consultant dedicated to providing constant support to the staff and volunteers of the organization.

As I am sure you have realized by now, choosing the right consulting firm is the most important decision you can make when you decide to embark on a capital campaign.

I speak to a great many nonprofit organizations when they are considering retaining the services of our firm, and after they have asked most of their questions, I am nearly always asked, "What other questions should we be asking?" I think it is a great question, and I welcome it because I believe it shows an initial level of trust and a willingness to accept advice from someone who has been doing fundraising for over thirty years.

I always tell nonprofit leaders with whom I am meeting what I believe they should ask when considering partnering with a development and fundraising consulting firm.

Any firm you interview should understand and know how to address the special circumstances that come with raising money and conducting capital campaigns for your specific organization.

The first question I advise nonprofit committees to ask is, "How do we even find firms to interview?" While you can look online and do some preliminary research to find a few firms to interview, it might be more beneficial to call around to area nonprofits that have done campaigns and ask for recommendations. You can call members of other nonprofit boards or a regional development office and ask if there is a firm they recommend you use. If your organization is religiously affiliated, you can reach out to your denominational office and ask what other firms your denomination has used and had positive experience with in fundraising efforts. However, in the end, there are no shortcuts to finding the right firm. You will have to choose from a few recommended firms and interview them to see which method best suits your organization's expectations.

Before you conduct the interview, it is important for you to visit the firm's website to learn a few things about them. This way, you will be better prepared to ask questions based on what you have learned. During the interview process, decide if the firm's approach is a good fit with your organization and determine whether part-time or full-time consulting best suits your needs. The following questions are useful to ask during the interview process.

1. Ask whether the firm provides full-time or part-time service. In a follow-up question, ask the consultant which kind of service he or she believes to be superior. If the representative from the firm does not think the service his or her firm offers is superior, ask why it is offered.

2. You can also ask questions that indicate that you have done your research. For instance, you may say, "Full-time, on-site consulting offers daily on-site support to all staff and volunteers. In addition, it will generally raise significantly more funds. Do your clients enjoy the same support and financial achievement?" This question will force the representative from the firm to address the difference between part-time and full-time firms head on.

3. It is also helpful to ask about the average length of a campaign for an organization your size. Ask how it compares to nonprofits of other sizes. Discuss factors that make your organization unique and ask the firm's representatives what factors drive whether a campaign is shortened or lengthened.

4. When you interview the consulting firm, it is imperative for you to ask whether your consultant will be available to you to meet your volunteer needs, or if you will have to arrange your volunteers around the day the consultant is scheduled to be on site at your organization. You need to know up front how to plan and schedule your campaign, and much of that rests on when your consultant will be available to you. You should ensure that if the schedule changes at the last minute, the consultant will be flexible to work with you.

5. You should also ask the firm's representative, "What are the fees and costs associated with retaining your services?" and "Are there any hidden costs we need to know about?"

6. To show that you have also done your research, you can ask the representative, "Do you feel that there is a value to your participation in a readiness assessment/feasibility study before the campaign begins or do you think we could do one on our own?" If the representative says that his or her firm will conduct the assessment/survey, ask if the organization's leadership needs to be involved. Ask whether the firm prefers more personal interviews or more group meetings and how your consultant would structure these meetings. Once you have gotten your answer to this question, you can also ask if the firm helps you prior to the readiness assessment/feasibility study, or if you should anticipate preparing on your own until the consultant arrives for the first meeting. Also, make sure to ask about the cost for the preliminary work provided by the consulting firm, assuming the firm does preliminary work.

7. Finally, before you end the meeting, make sure you ask the representative this question: "What is the number one reason we should choose your firm? Is it the amount of money you raise, the impact your service has on the volunteers, or the length of the campaign?"

I admit that some of these are trick questions. However, how a firm answers these questions is very telling of the service it will provide to your organization when conducting your campaign.

After hearing the difference in the types of service offered, you must decide how much time and effort you can expect your board members, staff, and volunteers to contribute to the administration of the campaign.

No matter what any consulting firm tells you, someone at the organization is going to be responsible for the campaign 100 percent of the time. If you have a full-time consultant, your organization's leaders or administrator will not be the one drafting letters, training volunteers, picking up brochures, and contacting speakers; the consultant is doing that work. Some firms will encourage you to hire an additional staff person to assist in the campaign. Nevertheless, this ultimately means that you will be paying the consulting firm to instruct you on how to add to your staff. Between the part-time firm's fee and the salary of a new and inexperienced employee, this tends to be the costliest way to conduct a campaign.

After over thirty years in development, I now see three types of development consulting firms: those who offer full-time and on-site support, those who offer full-time support from a remote site, and those who offer part-time support.

A full-time, on-site development consulting firm places a consultant at the location of the nonprofit client. These consultants essentially move into a community and become part of the organization's staff for a predetermined period of time. A full-time consultant is the go-to individual for all purposes during the period of time an organization engages the firm.

Another option is to hire a full-time consultant who works from a remote location. These consultants work from their office and make themselves available to their client organizations over the phone, through email, and on a predetermined number of site visits. This consultant may be working on eight to ten nonprofit projects at a given time.

A third option is to engage the services of a part-time consultant, which leaves the bulk of the work of administering the capital campaign to nonprofit staff and volunteers. A part-time consultant may visit the organization once per month, although the number of visits can be negotiated during the contract negotiation process. You can hire a part-time consultant, whom you are paying $2,500 to $5,000 per day plus expenses, to fly back and forth as needed. However, if you haven't been through a campaign before and aren't certain of the exact needs, how will you know to call the consultant before the campaign is in real trouble?

Aren't you hiring an experienced consultant so that he or she can tell you what is needed and anticipate problems? If a part-time firm says that it can manage your campaign in six on-site visits, when you divide the fee by the number of visits at your school, you can be paying $20,000 or more per visit.

In my experience, engaging the services of a full-time, on-site consultant is the most cost-effective way to conduct a capital campaign. It is also important to find a consulting firm that provides teaching in practical development growth skills to the volunteers involved in the campaign. Their mission is to use those skills to teach others.

While the challenges remain the same in all capital campaigns, I am finding a growing urgency in the need to conduct the campaigns immediately and to maximize results.

The number of people looking to become involved in your organization is rising and may be straining the ability of the staff and facilities. There continues to be competition for the best programs. Prospective participants are searching for the best experience or learning opportunity available. Nonprofits are constantly competing for new members. It is important that your organization offers the very best and most well-rounded environment and experience. This will also include the facilities you utilize, whether it be a theater, event space, office environment, or otherwise. It is important that your organization projects the most impressive image to all prospective participants. In addition, this image of success is important for your constituency, current financial supporters, and prospective donors. There are many successful nonprofit campaigns going on all over the country right now. If you conduct your campaign properly, you can be successful in any economy.

If your organization is considering a capital campaign, you owe it to the nonprofit leaders and volunteers to provide the necessary support to ensure success. Whether you are embarking on yet another phase of a multiphase building project or this is the first campaign your organization has conducted in fifty years, it is imperative that your project be successful. Deciding on the right consulting firm with which to partner is as important as deciding to conduct a campaign in the first place. The wrong decision and the wrong consultant can prove to be one of the costliest mistakes your organization can make.

MAIN MESSAGE

Selecting the right consulting firm is crucial to the success of a Capital Campaign. The decision must be made as to whether a full-time or part-time consulting firm can offer the appropriate support to all campaign volunteers and staff to ensure success.

CHAPTER 14

Estate Giving: How Planned Giving Can Be Included in a Capital Campaign

I am often asked about including estate giving—also referred to as *planned giving*—with the needs of a nonprofit capital campaign. While estate giving is an extremely important aspect of a nonprofit organization's continued financial security, you must have a specific strategy when including it, and it must only be used when speaking with certain members of your constituency.

The needs of the organization will determine how planned giving can be included in a campaign. Usually, since planned giving cannot be tied to a specific or determined timeline for a donation, it is included in an endowment campaign. However, many campaigns are now including scholarship opportunities or even capital reserve accounts. These needs can be specifically funded by an estate gift.

In other words, an urgent need—such as replacing the roof on a deteriorating building—cannot wait for a planned gift to fund the project. When there is an immediate concern, capital campaigns seek funds that will be pledged and paid in the near future. A new HVAC system is another such expenditure that must be addressed quickly; it cannot wait for a donation that the organization may not receive for years, if not decades.

In addition to the timing of funding a particular project, planned giving should be reserved and only used selectively for another reason. If planned giving is used as a "sales tool" during a particular capital campaign, it can serve as a temptation for all donors to give in that manner (that is, planned giving), rather than during the three-to-five-year pledge period. I strongly believe—and always advise—that planned giving be considered by prospective donors who are in their seventies, eighties, or nineties. Far too often, a prospective donor in their fifties or sixties may make an estate gift to an institution. While it is a good and generous commitment, too many obstacles can arise during the following several decades. I am certainly not advising that you resist these donations; I am simply stating that it may not be prudent to count on these gifts for many decades, if at all. It can be dangerous to start spending the funds pledged before they have been collected, and that is especially true when considering estate gifts, considering the many variables that exist.

Again, it is important not to use planned giving as a "sales tool" unless you are prepared to accept it from a larger portion of your constituency than you ever thought possible. Additionally, if the needs of your organization are urgent or immediate, it is far more important to request that your financial supporters fund these needs in the immediate future instead of providing long-term gifts.

During a campaign I directed years ago, the Executive Director and I visited an elderly supporter of the organization. We explained the need to purchase property adjoining the existing building in order to provide for future expansion. We made a request for a gift of $1 million. The woman was very supportive of the need and explained that she would always be in favor of expansion. However, she was in her nineties and was uncertain of the expenses and healthcare costs she would face in the coming years. She offered to contribute $500,000 immediately to be used toward the purchase of the property. However, she requested that the remaining $500,000 be paid by her estate at the time of her passing. Naturally, the Executive Director and I were not only grateful for the commitment but touched by the sentiment and her support for the organization. One week later, we received a letter from her attorney with a financial commitment for the second half of her gift to be paid by her estate. Naturally, the gift was counted in its entirety for the purposes of the campaign and, more importantly, to give this supporter recognition for making such a generous commitment to the organization. Sadly, our wonderful benefactor passed a couple of years later. As promised, the remaining $500,000 was paid to the organization promptly. We were all delighted that we were able to honor this wonderful supporter in her lifetime.

MAIN MESSAGE

Estate giving, or planned giving, should be used selectively based on the particular situation of prospective donors. It should also be focused on specific but not necessarily urgent and immediate needs of the organization.

CHAPTER 15
Get Your Organization Out of Debt

The number of nonprofit organizations around the United States that carry significant debt is growing every day. It is not an overstatement to say that it is reaching epidemic proportions. Years ago, most prospective clients who called my firm called regarding the need to raise funds for new construction, renovation, and property acquisition. However, these days most calls to our firm to discuss needs include the need to reduce debt. There are many reasons nonprofits may be in debt. Some organizations have used a line of credit to pay for deferred maintenance issues; some have construction loans; others purchased property for future expansion that is now on hold.

I must confess that I do not like nonprofit indebtedness at all. There is certainly no economic advantage to a nonprofit organization being in debt for an extended period of time. However, nonprofit leaders often tell me that they believe debt for any organization, including their own, is a good thing. I can understand the viewpoint of making the organization's constituency—including the donors—feel needed through their continued financial support. I can even understand the desire to make current members feel a challenge to support new opportunities in the organization of which they are a part. However, when the debt reaches a point where the current budget cannot sustain the payments, or the loan payments significantly impact the current programs, I have a difficult time seeing the good in that debt. When 40 to 50 percent of a nonprofit's budget is earmarked for debt payments, it undermines the institution's financial stability and handicaps the organization's ability to do more and provide better opportunities for its members and the community. It can undermine the confidence both current and past donors have in the organization's leadership, including the board and administration.

One nonprofit that was deeply in debt had to substantially eliminate staff and cut vital programs and services in order to compensate. The current members and staff were understandably unhappy. They voiced their disapproval by cutting their financial support for the organization, which negatively affected the annual budget. Some members even left.

There are two paths that nonprofit leaders should consider, and they are not mutually exclusive. One involves more focused attention on the annual campaign. Ensure that most of your constituency is at least pledging annually to the organization. The second consideration involves educating your constituency about the organization's debt and conducting a focused and intense capital campaign to try to retire the debt in a five-year period. Begin with a series of focus group meetings and personal interviews that educate and inspire support for the campaign. Engage the members of the entire community and current financial supporters in discussions of how the debt is influencing the annual budget.

My firm is currently working with a nonprofit that considered using our services nine years ago for a new building project. After much deliberation, the organization's leaders made the decision not to use outside counsel and conducted the campaign on their own. Unfortunately, with little focus and direction, the campaign was unsuccessful. However, when the time came to make the decision to move forward, they voted to build the new $10 million facility in spite of the poor results yielded by the campaign. As the years progressed, the organization amassed $360,000 in annual debt service for the new building. After a full nine years of debt service, the leaders once again contacted my firm to help retire the debt. This time, they understood that hiring good and experienced counsel was an investment, not an expense. I only wish they would have conducted the campaign properly from the beginning. It would have saved the organization well over $3 million in debt service alone.

These funds could have been used much more effectively for the support of staff, programming opportunities, scholarships, and even endowment. So while I often hear arguments that debt is good for a nonprofit, I always counter that a properly run campaign is far better in the long term.

MAIN MESSAGE

Even if your debt is so large that you think it will take generations to retire it, it is this generation's responsibility to do their part now.

CHAPTER 16
Collection Loss in Pledges

I recently presented the services of our firm to a large nonprofit organization in Southern California. The presentation went well, and I was asked many questions regarding full-time and on-site consulting.

Toward the end of the presentation, one question that I often get came up: "How much can we expect donors to pay on pledges?" Having been down this road many times before, I knew what the person was actually asking was, "What type of collection loss can we expect from the total amount pledged to the capital campaign?" In other words, how many pledges will actually be honored?

My standard response, after thirty years of fundraising consulting, is to say that usually between 96 percent and 98 percent of the money pledged during a campaign is actually received. Very often, nonprofit campaigns continue to visit donors during the three-to-five-year pledge period, and during those visits, they raise more money than was originally pledged at the start of the campaign.

After I answered, several individuals began speaking at the same time. They explained that in their previous campaign, only 60 percent of the pledged funds were realized. When I asked how the campaign was conducted, they explained that the fundraising firm they had hired strongly believed in asking prospective donors to give in group solicitation meetings, which usually took the form of cocktail parties with a dinner included. Before the end of the event, a request was made for pledges of a particular amount. Whether the amount requested was $10,000, $25,000, or $100,000, the point is that a large request had been made publicly. The sad truth is that while some supporters may have the ability to make such a pledge, it is usually not taken seriously, as the method of the request is so impersonal. The other concern is that some donors may feel so much pressure to make the requested pledge at the time of the request that they do so even if they do not have the financial ability to honor such a gift later on.

Unfortunately, group solicitation is the worst way to conduct a capital campaign effort. Fundraising firms that employ this type of technique usually only provide part-time consulting. They do not have the time or ability to work daily with the nonprofit client and volunteers or to personally visit all prospective donors. Their only opportunity to make requests is during large public events. While this is certainly easier for the consulting firm, it is always the worst way to secure meaningful pledges from prospective donors who feel the impersonal nature of the request.

In addition, it is very important to honor confidentiality in a capital campaign. All donors should be treated with respect and offered the opportunity for a personal meeting in order to ask questions and openly discuss the needs of the organization. Only then should a donor be asked to consider a pledge to the capital campaign.

The other reason our clients enjoy a higher than average collection on capital campaign pledges is due to quarterly progress reports and financial giving statements of a donor's commitment and payments. A constant progress report on the new construction, renovation, debt elimination, or anything else the campaign effort is addressing is important to share with your constituency. Every donor wants to know that their giving is being used effectively and that it is being used for the purpose agreed upon at the time of the commitment. These progress reports can be made via letter, email, newsletters, public announcements, or any other method that is an effective way to share the news that funds are being use for their intended purpose.

A quarterly statement to all donors is important as a reminder of a donor's pledge and continued commitment. The reason I prefer quarterly statements is to give supporters time to make necessary arrangements to honor an annual pledge. Quarterly reminders are both helpful and unobtrusive, and many prospective donors appreciate the follow-up.

Recently, I was speaking to the administrator of a nonprofit in Washington, DC. We discussed statements for pledges, and he admitted that the only statements they send out are sent at the end of the year. I asked if he felt that was enough time for a donor to catch up with payments if they had fallen behind. He acknowledged that it certainly was not enough time, but the idea of sending out quarterly statements had never occurred to anyone at the organization. I concealed my surprise and counseled him to begin quarterly statements; he appreciated the advice.

Sometimes a gentle reminder every few months can mean the difference between a donor making timely payments toward a pledge or making an apology for not being able to pay a pledge during the time agreed to during the campaign effort.

MAIN MESSAGE

If your organization wants to reduce the collection loss in pledges, treat donors with respect and honor them by performing one-on-one personal visits and providing quarterly progress reports and giving statements.

CHAPTER 17
Parting Thoughts

As I prepared to write *Fundraising: After the Pandemic*, I felt there were many common misconceptions regarding fundraising during this challenging time that needed to be addressed and shared with everyone involved with a nonprofit organization. Topics such as methods of fundraising, types of fundraising consulting firms, how to request support from prospective donors, and how statements of payments toward multiyear pledges should be administered were all things that needed to be considered.

In writing this book, my desire was simply to offer perspective and suggestions based on my thirty years of fundraising consulting. Having been in this business for so long has given me the ability to unequivocally say that there are no shortcuts in effective development for nonprofit organizations. This is especially true following a global pandemic. Now, more than ever, organizations need to know that you are on their side and in their corner, giving it all you have to help them achieve their goals, particularly during difficult economic times. The reason thousands of our past clients have been successful is primarily because of the deep and basic belief that all donors should be treated in the same manner and with respect. However, being open and honest regarding the needs of the organization is just the beginning. Taking that information to leaders—both past and present—creating ownership in all aspects of the organization's constituency, and respectfully requesting community consideration to support these needs is the basic blueprint for success.

In addition, there are a few overarching points I want everyone to take away from this book.

First, find a fundraising partner—someone who will serve as a project manager and coach—someone who will be with you every step of the way. Find someone who can be objective about the needs and vision you have and not someone who is solely driven by monetary gains or compensated by a percentage of the funds raised.

Second, do not let anyone tell you what you can or cannot raise. You will read stories of schools, churches, and other nonprofit organizations that raised significantly more than they ever dreamed possible by using our method. You will also hear about other institutions that used another method and could not raise enough to even cover a kick-off campaign event. Every case is different. The leadership of the organization and a well-implemented, proven plan are essential to succeed. On that note, let me reiterate that the cause of the campaign (or the case for support) can affect the level of giving. You may have the greatest consultant in the world with a great plan, but if the focus of the campaign is to raise money to pay off a debt you acquired from overbuilding and poor planning from the last campaign, it could be a challenge. Even with the best campaign plan, raising a modest amount could be viewed as an incredible accomplishment for a campaign where the sole purpose is debt reduction.

Third, do not start recruiting your campaign committee before selecting your fundraising consultant. Just as you would not hire an electrician to wire your home before you hired the architect to design it, putting the cart before the horse, campaign-wise, only confuses matters.

Fourth, after you hire your consultant, listen to him or her. You are paying for his or her experience and expertise; do not let your money go to waste by assuming that you know better.

Fifth, there is never a best time to conduct a campaign, but there are times that are better than others. Do not let the economy or world events affect the needs that you have identified. If the needs are important to the organization and the community, the constituency will support them.

Finally, let me say that conducting a successful campaign is more important than the amount of money raised. When people feel that they are part of something worthwhile and successful, the effort will be remembered and even cherished. Your organization and its leaders should enjoy a reawakening and resurgence when all of your organization's supporters work together toward a common goal and provide important and necessary opportunities for future generations and the community. That being said, do not set a goal that you cannot reach. Listen to your consultant; he or she should advise you to determine a reasonable goal, which you can then achieve or even surpass!

Please do not attempt a campaign on your own unless you have very modest needs. If that is the case, I hope I have convinced you that with a little effort, a bit of research, and a great deal of dedication, you could raise that on your own without outside counsel. For everything else, I hope I can help you find the right firm for your organization.

Thank you for reading and I wish you great success on your journey.

www.ingramcontent.com/pod-product-compliance
Lightning Source LLC
Chambersburg PA
CBHW040858210326
41597CB00029B/4890